Understanding Human Behavior in 2019

The Complete Guide to Mastering the Art of Analyzing People, Body Language, Persuasion, Behavioral Psychology and Ethical Manipulation

Written by John Berkowitz

© **Copyright 2019 John Berkowitz - All rights reserved.**

The content contained within this book may not be reproduced, duplicated or transmitted without direct written permission from the author or the publisher.

Under no circumstances will any blame or legal responsibility be held against the publisher, or author, for any damages, reparation, or monetary loss due to the information contained within this book. Either directly or indirectly.

Legal Notice:

This book is copyright protected. This book is only for personal use. You cannot amend, distribute, sell, use, quote or paraphrase any part, or the content within this book, without the consent of the author or publisher.

Disclaimer Notice:

Please note the information contained within this document is for educational and entertainment purposes only. All effort has been executed to present accurate, up to date, and reliable, complete information. No warranties of any kind are declared or implied. Readers acknowledge that the author is not engaging in the rendering of legal, financial, medical or professional advice. The content within this book has been derived from various sources. Please consult a licensed professional before attempting any techniques outlined in this book.

By reading this document, the reader agrees that under no circumstances is the author responsible for any losses, direct or indirect, which are incurred as a result of the use of information contained within this document, including, but not limited to, — errors, omissions, or inaccuracies.

Table Of Contents

Introduction 7

Chapter 1: The Art of Analyzing People 11

    The Three Components of Human Behavior . 15

    Analyzing and Deciphering Behavioral Patterns 25

    Body Language 27

    Tips and Tricks for Analyzing Body Language 37

Chapter 2: The Subtle Art of Persuasion 48

    The Steps of Persuasion 50

    How to Influence People 58

    Manipulating the Power and Freedom of Will (Willpower and Free Will) 69

    The Art of Subtle Manipulations 73

Chapter 3: Using the Knowledge of Human Psychology to Your Advantage (Tips and Tricks) 76

Chapter 4 : The Driving Force of Human Behavior (Motivation)..89

    The Driving Factors of Motives 91

    Classification of Motivation........................... 97

Chapter 5: Human Behavior and Irrationality . 111

    Factors That Influence Irrational Behavior ..116

Chapter 6: Recognizing and Resisting Manipulation...121

    Why We Are Easily Manipulated 122

    Spotting Manipulation 128

    Resisting Manipulation 131

Chapter 7: Persuasion: Just How Wrong Is It? 136

    The Methods of Persuasion 138

Chapter 8: Where Do our Opinions Come From? 155

Chapter 9: Factors that Influence Human Behavior 160

   Propaganda Influences Us 164

   Patriotism Influences Us 167

   We are Influenced by Hate 168

   How to Conquer the Influence of Hate 171

Chapter 10: Fear and How to Overcome Its Influence 183

   Overcoming the Influence of Fear 186

Conclusion 199

Introduction

In recent times, much cognizance has been given to the patterns of human behavior so as to be able to aptly predict, decipher and understand the primary reasons for our actions, needs, and reactions. It is for this cause that the study of human behavior is essential, to not only a select few but to a wide range of persons, not limited to but inclusive of the following: Psychologists, economists, business and world leaders, amongst others. The psychologist needs an understanding of their client's behavior to proffer practical solutions better; the economist needs it to predict demand and supply more accurately, and all the many different forces that affect individuals, society, and exchange; and the business leaders need it to introduce new products and services to better meet their customers' needs and to drive profits. All these and more stem from the primary understanding of human behavior.

In this vein, human behavior can thus be

deduced to be mostly responsible for human interactions and indulgences, within and outside of our environment. What then is this term, 'human behavior?'

Human behavior refers to our reactions to stimulus (internal or external), needs, desires, etc., and all the voluntary or involuntary measures we undertake in order to attain a particular state. Human behavior spans across all the many different physical, emotional, and psychological responses particular to our efforts to survive in life.

However, although the different behaviors may vary across persons (what with the prevalence of particular personality types, differing preferences, various psychologies, and responses), a behavior is peculiar and distinct to all. This distinction arises from the change in behavioral patterns undergone by an individual as they transition through ages and tripartite states. This is a plausible example of how an adult behaves differently from a teenager and a baby, but are not all, in themselves, bereft of behavior.

The behavior of human beings further increases in importance as it serves a means of adequately deducing the human mind and thought process or pattern, feelings, and attitudes of a ubiquitous quality. This relative importance forms the basis for which these behaviors are categorized based, on their acceptability, prevalence, rarity, unacceptability, et al. These ranges of categorization are most often influenced by social, ethnic, genetic, ethical, personal, imposed (personal or by another party), and religious interactions that serve to spur an individual into a given path of thoughts, actions and, subsequently, behavioral patterns. This is why human behavior plays a pivotal role in determining how an individual turns out, their choices, and desires.

And, as much as human behavior has gathered much acclaim in contemporary times, which has made it subject to study, results have shown that it is indeed subject to willpower and genius, even—that is, contradictory to the typical stereotype of human behavior being somewhat too complicated and incapable of being understood, it has been proven that human behavior can be harnessed, tweaked, and exploited.

This book expressly captures human behavior in its essence, baring its susceptibilities, strengths, and driving power. It teaches how to ably put behavioral patterns to use and make the most of them. This book achieves this by the impartation of knowledge that can provide the reader with an accurate understanding of human behavioral patterns. Albeit, as a disclaimer, although this book teaches how to bend human behavior to the reader's advantage, it is in no way promoting the act of exploitation. As such, this knowledge is offered with the best of intention to be put to use positively and help with the goings on of everyday living.

Chapter 1: The Art of Analyzing People

The concept of human behavior revolves around three main components that determine the pattern of occurrences undergone by an individual. These three components are: Emotion, action, and cognition. They form the primary medium of expression an individual uses to communicate feelings, reactions, and meanings in particular situations. All three components, although common to every person, can vary quite dramatically.

Human behavior can be used as a medium of analyzing a person and deducing conclusive evidence, or in some cases near accurate predictions, of their characteristics. And, although a host of factors may influence human behavior at a particular point in time, what with the ever-flexible nature it portrays, the analysis of this behavior in that one moment tells much about the person exhibiting such characteristics.

Also, since human behavior is particular to persons in varying measures, it better helps tell people apart. As such, behavior is most often a pivotal part of any human classification, be it based on temperance, likes, dislikes, or reactions, as examples.

This flexibility in the nature of human behavior stems from an individual's continued attempt at satisfying their physical, psychological, and emotional needs. Another contributing factor in this regard is the complexity and dynamic nature of the environment that flexes the individual's behavior as they seek to better interact and adapt to their surroundings. This results in an evolution in their physical, emotional, and psychological characteristics, which soon settles into a regular pattern of occurrence. This regularity in occurrence begets behavioral patterns.

Once any form of expression conveys a similar meaning, feeling, etc. in any same such situations over time, it forms a pattern. Simply put, a particular behavior repeatedly exhibited in the same scenarios makes for a behavioral model. Hence, behavioral patterns being attained now then become necessary to attach specific meanings to these patterns so as to be able to decode and understand them correctly.

These patterns then manifest into features such as habits, signs, body language, tone of voice, etc., with which an individual divulges their psychological, emotional, or physical conditions and their effects on third parties.

However, human behavior is not limited to physical interactions alone since its component makeup is mainly abstract. This accounts for the perception of human behavior as reaching beyond the conceivable consciousness to the subconscious.

The subconscious plays a significant role in the system of human behavior, influencing the formation of patterns and their relative meanings, which have, over time, been associated with real causal interactions. As such, the subconscious complements the conscious part of behavioral patterns in our interaction with our environment.

For instance, we would withdraw immediately from very hot objects no matter our age. No matter how much this action is repeated with the same individual or different persons, the reaction of recoiling is almost always the same. Thus, this conveys the behavioral pattern that a withdrawal reaction follows the handling of very hot objects. More so, the reaction doesn't necessarily involve giving cognizance to the purpose before withdrawal, as the response is impulsive and almost wholly devoid of volition.

This pattern gives rise to the conditions of voluntary and involuntary reactions, both of which complement the subconscious and conscious processes of human behavior. In this vein, does human behavior derive its complexity owing to the proximity shared by reaction conditions (voluntary and involuntary) and perceptive processes (conscious and subconscious)?

It is only by these qualities that human behavior can indeed be accurately analyzed, as it bares each part responsible for the patterns exhibited by an individual.

The Three Components of Human Behavior

First, let us consider the founding components of human behavior, as there, indeed, can be no behavioral pattern whatsoever without them.

Behavioral Actions:

The actions of an individual form one of the anchor components of their behavior. It could mean every other indulgence of the individual that isn't beyond notice is in their perceptive consciousness. That is, the actions of an individual as behavior can be perceived by sight or any of the other physiological senses.

Actions serve to put into motion a translation from one phase to another. They are the bases upon which change is attained and a pattern made traceable. On this account, it can thus be deduced that actions are proximal to time and change. As such, behavioral action progresses across a timeframe, initiating a series of change on, and by, the individual.

Primarily, behavioral actions are divided into two forms, which are voluntary and involuntary actions. These forms take on a repeated pattern, or occurrence, around which the overall action is perceived and forthwith adjudged. Examples of behavioral actions range from voluntary indulgences, such as feeding, sleeping, and using the muscles, to involuntary activities, such as sweating, sneezing, and blinking, etc.

In the voluntary action of feeding, the individual makes a conscious effort at eating: Indulging the muscles of the arm in moving the food towards the mouth and the jaws in the digestion of the food. In this action, the continuous movement of the arm to the mouth and the movements of the jaw forms the pattern termed 'feeding,' or 'eating.' It is, for this reason, any such alike model would be considered as eating.

On the other hand, the spontaneous action of blinking, is almost entirely void of the individual's volition, in some cases. One of these such cases would be the approaching of an external object near the eye. The eyelids, in this case, would shut instinctively to protect the eyes from damage faster than it would take the individual to process and react to the object. And, when this impulsiveness continues in similar scenarios, a pattern is formed. These, put together, connote the individual's behavioral actions in these different scenarios and can be interpreted as feeding and as defensive techniques, employed to aptly satisfy both the individual and the need at the particular moment.

Behavioral Cognition:

The cognitive aspect refers to the logic and activities of mental functionality. In this vein, behavioral cognition is related to the mental processes associated with thinking and imagining in an individual.

Like actions, behavioral cognition is of two necessary forms, namely: Non-verbal and verbal. The former is mainly characterized by the process of imagining or conjuring up images. It is a conscious mental effort undergone by an individual in picturing a phase of time either in the past or present. For instance, a child daydreams of how much fun they would have with a toy car promised to them by a parent. In this instance, the child projects himself into the future mentally and wordlessly, exercising control over the outcome of their imagination. Non-verbal cognition, as the name connotes, is a mental process bereft of any written or spoken communication and mainly involving expressions such as gestures, signs, and body language.

As such, non-verbal cognition involves a series of behavioral patterns aimed at communicating the feelings, moods, etc. of an individual, without the need for speaking and/or writing.

Verbal cognition, on the other hand, indicates the thought processes that are categorized by words. Verbal cognition often takes the form of a monologue, mental notes, or musings. No words might be said, but thoughts are indeed construed with a measure of relativity to a subject matter. An example of this could include making a mental note to get something or musings on what another person might think of you. In both cases, there is no projection of images, but a thought pattern revolving around saving the information and critiquing the thoughts of another person.

Behavioral cognition spans to include specific knowledge and skill set that is useful to the mental processes of storing and scrutinizing information. It exists in both the subconscious and conscious realms since thoughts and imaginations are abstract but perceivable, nonetheless. The behavioral cognition is responsible for the flexibility of interaction between an individual and their immediate environment. As such, it is because of cognitive behavior that an individual can perform tasks to a commendable extent and to comport themselves to attain a particular goal. This accounts for why an individual is able to memorize and think in a way that creates workable solutions.

Behavioral Emotion:

The emotions of an individual are the internal states that trigger involuntary reactions in their physiology. These instinctive reactions originate from perceptive data and physical sources as responses to contact with tangible concepts, such as situations or objects.

Emotions could also refer to an experience of conscious perceptions that stem from robust mental processes for a brief period of time. However, its conscious nature is limited to its perception and expression alone because it results from neither knowledge nor reasoning. This connotes that emotions are somewhat abstract or hidden from the perception of sight.

Behavioral emotions exist in two primary forms: Positive and negative. The former indicates any experience which is considered useful, pleasurable, and desirable. On the other hand, the latter denotes experiences that are bad, unpleasant, and undesirable. An example of positive behavioral emotions is a feeling of excitement over a particular situation. In this case, the emotion brings desirables qualities of happiness and a sense of joy. An example of negative emotion is grief; to any extent, the sense of bereavement has a least desirable quality that makes an individual less likely to want to experience it again.

Furthering on, emotional behavior denotes the way in which an individual reacts in varying emotional states and all the decisive measures taken to defeat or retain the emotion. However, behavioral emotions span across mental perceptions to include physiological responses to emotions. Some examples of these physiological responses include perspiration, accelerated heart and respiration rates, and arousals.

And, since emotions are similar to cognition in their abstract nature, they cannot be sensed with the eyes but can be spotted by closely observing signs, such as facial expressions, excitement levels, skin reactions (such as goosebumps), breathing intensity, for instance. These make up the way in which the individual manages their emotions and how they are affected by them.

Now that the three components of human behavior have been considered, cognizance can be given to how they combine to determine the overall behavior of an individual.

The behavioral actions, emotions, and cognition may share a distinction from one another, but not one makes up the overall behavior of a person independently. As such, they are combined to give a definite sense to human behavior, denoting the way they sense, and respond to, their surroundings, interact with others, think of and create solutions or answers, listen to inner musings, and imagine a future and work towards it, as examples. The interdependence of all three components results in the phenomenon of cause and effect, which is yet to be given specific roots; this is due to varying actions that would be responded to in many different ways.

Answering the door and being surprised by a friend you haven't seen in a long while is an example of the interdependence of all three components. The action here is in answering the door, the emotion is one of surprise and, predictably, joy, and the cognition is of recognizing the friend and noting the timeframe since you last met. In this case, all three components work together to express that you, although surprised at the unplanned visit, are nonetheless happy to see them. This already defines this particular behavior as easygoing. This case also shows the action as being the primary reason that results in the emotion and cognition, because if the action had not been performed, neither the emotion nor the cognition would have been triggered. That is, action = emotion (surprise and/or joy) and cognition (long lost friend)

In buttressing the point of the cause and effect phenomenon, it could happen that the cognition and emotion might be different, even when the action remains the same. In this case, the emotion might vary from being alarmed, to anxious, to uninterested, while the cognition might be an inability to identify who the visitor is. Hence, for this case, the cause (action) precedes the effects (cognition and emotion).

In cases where the phenomenon of cause and effect undergoes a change in sequence, the action is more likely to be the resulting condition of the cognitive and emotional processes. An example of this is when you continuously muse about a failed relationship and begin to feel depressed but avert it by going out with friends. Here, the behavioral cognition (a failed relationship) links to a resulting emotion (depression) and combine together to trigger the behavioral action (going out). In essence, the action of going out was triggered by the emotional feeling of depression and the primary causal agent, cognition. That is, the cognition (musing about the failed relationship) and relative emotion (feeling of depression) = action (going out with friends).

On analysis, this behavioral sequence shows the individual taking evasive actions to avoid a breakdown (emotion) and overthinking (cognition).

Analyzing and Deciphering Behavioral Patterns

Having considered the basic components of

human behavior (cognition, emotion, and action), we shall now consider behavioral patterns.

Behavioral patterns arise from the regular repetition of a particular behavior in a continuous sequence of synonymous scenarios. That is, a behavioral pattern is attained when an individual responds or interacts in a similar fashion to the same scenarios repeatedly. This, of course, is exclusive of diminishing interest and the timeframe of the repetitive scenario.

Behavioral patterns convey non-verbal meanings such as the feelings, moods, and interests of an individual. It is for this reason they have been shown to account for a considerable percentage of communication processes, leaving their verbal opposite with just 7% of the contribution. To this acclaim, a proper knowledge of non-verbal behavior is important if the human behavior is to be properly analyzed and extracted of its meanings. These may vary across individuals, owing to the differences in psychological and physical responses, but some common ones do exist. On this account, their analyses bear close proximities in meaning.

Behavioral patterns common to everyday activities are inclusive, but not limited to, the following:

Body Language

This is, arguably, the most widely-perceived behavioral pattern, and the easiest to recognize and decipher. Body language exists in an almost homogeneous pattern across individuals with very little differences owing to variations.

Body language can be defined as any non-verbal expression employed by the body as a means of conveying a message. This message is usually in the form of cognitive and emotional messages that an individual chooses, for some reason, in order to not communicate verbally.

Body language constitutes a major part of human

interaction and can offer proficient information about the character of an individual. For instance, an individual can be classified as proud if he or she expresses body languages such as raising their nose in the air and carrying the body haughtily. Also, studies suggest that effusive body language during communication portrays that the information being given out is genuine, while a communication with little to no body language and shifty eyes is likely to be false. This portrays just how much body language appears as a major embodiment of the overall human behavior.

Body language accounts for a great deal of everyday communication as it helps bolster interaction and can be used to deduce the authenticity of the interaction. This is due to body language making up for what verbal communication lacks in the passing on of information.

Research has shown that body language makes up about 50 to 70 percent of human interaction between individuals and their environment. It is, for this reason, why the study of body language is of high importance since it offers an insight into the process in which people make effective communication. As such, an in-depth understanding of body language is key to deciphering the non-verbal hints made by people during an interaction.

Body language spans across many different cues and is not limited to bodily actions alone. It could include contexts that are otherwise almost beneath notice. That is, body language could more often than not exist as a series of signals rather than an outright action, conveying the cognitive and emotional conditions of an individual. Examples of such signals could include the direction of the feet, the behavior of the eyes, the pattern of sitting, sighs, posture, and disposition. These denote an individual's response during an interaction, offering an insight into their emotions and thoughts during the course of the interaction.

Some body languages common to everyday

perception are inclusive, but not limited to, the following:

1. Eye Motion:

In every verbal and non-verbal interaction, the position and movement of the eyes are important in helping to convey information. As such, the eyes give off the primary response of an individual during the interaction. The eyes may convey perceivable messages such as disinterest, boredom, disbelief, and anger. In essence, the eyes are but a mirror of an individual's nature and truest response.

Owing to this telling nature of the eyes, an understanding of this body language is effective in deciphering human behavior. As such, cognizance should be taken by the direction of the eyes, noting if it is direct and intense or wandering and fleeting. Study has shown that the inability to maintain direct eye contact could be interpreted as disinterest, dishonesty, boredom, or deception. This is especially the case when their gaze is directed sideways or away. A downwards gaze, on the other hand, may be a sign of respect, submission, or nervousness. Studies also reveal pupil dilation as a body language that indicates focus, a favorable response, or a cognitive effort. Pupil dilation is rather more difficult to ascertain if cognizance was never given to the size of the pupil previously. As such, cognizance should be given to the pupils during an interaction to successfully notice the enlargement.

Another eye-related condition is the rate of blinking. And, while blinking is an involuntary action and over-blinking could be the result of a medical condition, this small action could convey a message when it is neither of the aforementioned. The rate of blinking conveys the internal cognitive or emotional state of a person. Hence, a person is more likely to blink more when feeling stressed or overthinking things. It could also mean falsehood and is likely to be accompanied by touching parts of the face, such as the eyes and mouth.

Also, a routine glance at an object could also connote the desirability of said object. For instance, a continued glance at the window could indicate a desire to be outside or to open the window. If the object is a person, it could mean a desire to talk to the individual or to keep them in sight. Studies also suggest that glancing in multiple directions could indicate either the truth or falsehood; glancing upwards and to the left connotes that the truth is being spoken, while glancing upwards and to the right connotes falsehood. Although this seems a rather weird fact, studies have shown that looking upwards and to the right denotes that an individual has no actual memory of the story. On the other hand, looking upwards and to the left indicates that the story is an actual retelling of a true memory.

In conclusion, people are more likely to glance at others based on the likable traits they exude. This also accounts for persons in higher positions, as highly-placed people have a greater tendency of being glanced at than those 'below' them.

2. Appearance (Dress Sense):

Someone's dress sense is the consciousness given to their manner of appearance. This stems from the reason why their appearance speaks more about their personality. It indicates how these people feel and what they want out of any interaction(s) they make. As such, their mode of conveying these messages is by appearing in ways peculiar to their distinct personalities and messages. The maxim, 'dress how you want to be addressed' quite buttresses this point.

For instance, appearing in a tank top and joggers indicates that an individual engages in exercise; a suit or tux on shined shoes indicates formality, success oriented, or ambition; a tight top baring cleavage on a skirt sitting above the knee could indicate attention-seeking or a salacious nature; trousers tucked into a shirt could indicate a casual air as would a T-shirt on jean trousers.

3. Proximity:

Proximity indicates the measure of distance between two people during interaction and as a body language in determining the behavior between people. Research shows close proximity during an interaction, such as standing or sitting, to indicate a good rapport. However, a distant proximity might indicate friction, fear, objection, or a lack of mutual rapport, as examples. As such, it is likely that an interaction is not taken in a homogeneous vein by two persons when one pulls further away or when the other draws near. For instance, a lady is more likely to keep a healthy distance from a man who makes inappropriate, unconsented advances towards her. This shows that both the lady and the man are not mutual in their interests.

Also, the measure of proximity could also indicate the type of relationship existing between them. For example, when two people are seen holding hands and maintaining a close proximity, it can be perceived that the relationship between them might range from friendship, to love, to family. However, a close proximity isn't necessarily an exact indicator of a relationship, especially when culture is concerned. For instance, in some cultures, people are supposed to join heads together and share a breath during greeting as a sign of oneness, whereas other cultures ban public displays of affection.

4. Head Movement:

The movement of the head during interaction is also a body language that could indicate a range of different behaviors, such as interest, impatience, focus, and patience. The nodding speed of an individual during interaction denotes their patience or impatience. A slower nodding speed denotes interest in an interaction and serves to bid a speaker on. On the other hand, faster nodding may denote disinterest, an unwillingness to listen further, or an indication that an individual wants a chance to speak as well. For instance, in an interaction between two individuals, one is talkative and the other is quite reserved; the latter is likely to nod somewhat ferociously as a sign that the former should quit talking and allow them to speak.

Also, a sideways inclination of the head could indicate rapt attention or interest during interaction while a backward inclination of the head indicates disbelief, doubt, or suspicion. A slight nod at someone could also serve as a sign of greeting or acknowledgment.

5. Arm Position:

A popular maxim has it that the arms are the doorways to the body. In this case, the measure of acceptance or reluctance is conveyed by the position of the arms during an interaction. Folding the arms across the chest indicates a gesture of defense, reluctance, vulnerability, narrow-mindedness, or anxiety. However, this body language could also connote positive attitudes such as confidence or relaxation, especially when followed by a reassuring smile.

Standing with arms akimbo could indicate a

bossy nature, stress, or fatigue. Studies suggest men employ this stance more than women as a sign of dominance. This pose is likely to indicate stress or fatigue when accompanied by a sigh or a rubbing of the temples.

However, the analysis of this body language is not entirely applicable to every individual due to differing cultural, physical, emotional, and cognitive standards. As such, people are likely to respond differently owing to these factors. In essence, this non-verbal cue is to be properly analyzed based on individual distinction.

Tips and Tricks for Analyzing Body Language

1. Open-mindedness:

When trying to analyze someone's body language, and garner information about their behaviors, being open-minded is key. This will provide a clearer, more indifferent means of receiving information so as to get a genuine translation of the intuitive, non-verbal hints communicated by others. But, this cannot be done with prejudice, sentiments, or stereotypes, which are only helpful in preventing a rational consideration of the person, thus leading to poorer perspectives and biased meanings. With this in mind, it is of high importance to maintain a sense of objectiveness and impartiality so as to be able to retrieve information fairly and without judgment. But, open-mindedness is not limited to being devoid of bias, sentiments, and stereotypes alone; it also involves bereaving oneself of archaic and finite perspectives that may inhibit the process of analysis.

Open-mindedness is an important factor in analyzing the behavioral patterns of people because there is little to no progress without it. This stems from the reason that open-mindedness offers an insight past any facade into the real behavioral persona of an individual. As such, maximum attention is given to the analysis of the dynamic nature of human behavior in differing conditions, rather than preconceived perceptions of what could be, but actually may not.

2. Intuition:

Sometimes, the subconscious carries out the probing of someone's behaviors and communicates them to us via intuitive feelings. These feelings are usually beyond the perceivable consciousness, arising mostly from the heightening of the senses. Intuition makes one capable of reaching another beyond the behavioral patterns and verbal communication they exhibit. It's almost like a communication of both parties on the subconscious level, with each of them analyzing the other and reporting to their consciousness.

Intuition is characterized by a gut feeling triggered by the senses rather than the cognitive processes of the head. As such, it is more of an instinctive response than a well-thought-out cognitive process. That is, intuition exists as non-verbal communication perceived through instincts, images, and bodily impulses, in lieu of logical reasoning.

Intuition, like open-mindedness, seeks for contacts beyond the outer facade of ourselves instead of the real behavioral pattern hidden away. As such, its approach of seeing beyond the perceivable results in a better and clearer analysis of someone's behavior.

3. Emotions:

Emotions cut deeper across human behavior than it is given credit for. It spans over both the conscious and subconscious and can arguably be dubbed as the most important indicator in analyzing someone. On the conscious front, emotions make use of the senses in perceiving the behavior of others. The subconscious, on the other hand, relies on impulsive responses characterized as intuition.

These prove that emotions are somewhat of a force to be reckoned with in analyzing behavioral patterns of people, as it is common to all and fosters interactions on both conscious and subconscious levels.

Emotions can be classified as an exhibition of the energy felt by people. This energy is usually in the forms of vibes and auras, which are only susceptible to subconscious detection, rather than moods and feelings, which are perceivable in the conscious. However, on both conscious and subconscious levels, emotions are only decipherable by intuition. This is because human nature, being dynamic in itself, might respond differently in a particular scenario over time due to the many different factors that could affect emotional state. Hence, no logic is thoroughly able to accurately analyze it.

Furthering on, emotions are only detectable and able to be analyzed by the energy they emit. This energy is capable of being perceived subconsciously during close contact with people, commonly known by its name in Chinese medical terminology, 'chi.' Chi accounts for the intuitive force of an individual, making it possible to access the true nature of others on a subconscious level.

An oppressor continually sees himself above the oppressed because the latter gives off an aura (chi) of fear and submission. The same is the case when you feel uneasy walking past a dangerous looking person and have the feeling of being watched. This simple action of proximity, which causes an increased heart rate and pace, stems from you perceiving the other person's chi as foreboding.

4. Hand Gestures or Signals:

The gestures or signals of the hand involves the motion of the arms during interaction as a means of emphasizing verbal communication (speech, especially). Gestures and signals serve as very important behavioral patterns owing to the directness of their nature. In essence, hand gestures are almost never faked. As such, the action of gestures are important in interaction and serve as a mode of conveying non-verbal cues about a person's behavior. These could range from the slightest wave, to pointing, to a type of handshake, as examples. All these and more suggest the true behavior of an individual during an interaction, baring their feelings at a particular moment.

However, unlike other behavioral patterns, hand gestures could stem from cultural as well as societal origins. For example, holding up the index finger and the second finger after the thumb is a sign of peace in some cultures. This, however, might not apply to all cultures, as the gesture might be meaningless or imply negativity.

Some common hand gestures peculiar to everyday interactions include the following:

The 'thumbs up' sign indicates to the receiver a positive acknowledgment. In some cases, it is interpreted as a 'power' thumb but the meaning is no different from the former. There exists a direct opposite of the thumbs up signal, which is 'thumbs down,' indicating disapproval.

Clenched fists is a sign with a variety of meanings depending on how and why it is done. During an interaction, it could be interpreted as anger; when the fists are being clenched and unclenched uncontrollably, it could indicate anxiety, panic, or fear; raised clenched fists is an outright indication of solidarity to a cause.

Another gesture with a meaning is that made by connecting the index finger and thumb in a circle, having the remaining three fingers stretched out. This gesture indicates being 'all right' or 'okay.' However, as it is with cultural differences, this signal also connotes a negative response in parts of Europe and South America. In parts of Europe, this signal means the receiver is nothing, literally translated as 'you ain't shit.' In South America, it is simply considered vulgar.

In the instance where one places their hands on their laps, on their head, behind their back, or in their pockets, this could suggest falsehood, anxiety or nervousness.

When one leans on the elbows, resting the head on intertwined or cupped palms indicates a gesture of offering the face. This gesture suggests that an individual is interested in the other during an interaction and is more than willing to continue the interaction. In the case where the head is supported by a propped up hand resting on the elbow on a platform, this gesture is likely to suggest interest and focus. This stems from the reason that the individual is attentive enough to want to keep the interaction alive and holds up their head to induce focus. Where the head is being supported by the elbows propped up on a surface, this suggests that a person is bored by an interaction or unwilling to listen any further.

Another non-verbal hand gesture is the blocking sign. This gesture indicates that a person is trying to put up a boundary or be defensive. It serves to keep the other party at an agreeable distance or, in some cases, keep themselves at bay from direct contact. This gesture is usually performed with an object, serving as the inhibitor between both parties.

Pointing with the finger could be a conscious or unconscious effort. If it's unconscious, it could suggest the pointer shares an attraction to the person being pointed at. This gesture spans to deduce the behavior of a person during an interaction, helping other parties understand whether or not a person is really interested in their interaction or faking it.

5. Voice Tone:

A final clue on analyzing behavioral patterns is their tone of voice during an interaction. The specific pitch and volume of voice used by a person gives off a non-verbal cue of their feelings, which could indicate varying feels, both positive and negative.

Since the tone of a person is conveyed by sound, and sound, in itself, is vibrations at particular frequencies, a person's tone is likely to have a direct effect on the listening party. This makes enables the listening party to be capable of deducing the behavior of the speaker, based on how the speaker's voice strikes them. For instance, a high pitch is likely to indicate anger, aggression, snappiness, or abrasiveness. A low pitch, on the other hand, could indicate a soothing nature, calmness, kindness, etc. A drawling pitch could indicate a whine, laziness, indecisiveness, tiredness, or unwillingness. A low, snappy voice pitch could indicate a haughty, bossy, or proud nature.

Chapter 2: The Subtle Art of Persuasion

At some time in our lives, we have all been at points when we badly needed to be able to change people's views and persuade them into buying our ideas, instead. However, there are more failures than successes at this endeavor, what with the variation in the way people respond, their thoughts, culture, and what they believe in. While these failures might sometimes only result in minimal penalties, this might not always be the case, especially when persuasive skills are a necessity. An example of this is in business; being unable to persuade and aptly convince people to procure a product or service is likely to have a negative impact on the business, especially if this is a regular occurrence.

As is the case with all scenarios requiring strong persuasive skills, one is expected to be adept enough in the study of human behavior to be better suited to flexing the willpower of people and using it to their advantage, thus making human behavior paramount in the quest to inquire into human nature and tweak the will.

Inference can thus be drawn into what persuasion denotes. Persuasion revolves around the process via which the behavior of a person is influenced by another person through communication rather than pressure. In essence, persuasion is a process of influencing a person's opinion and convincing them of another perspective. In other words, persuasion could indicate a manipulation of someone's will. While this might be seen as unethical, a school of thought is of the opinion that persuasion has a moral build-up, because it aids a sense of mutuality, social control, and brings about orderliness in society. Persuasion, thus, gains ground as a morally acceptable phenomenon rather than coercion and force. In essence, it is a lesser, necessary evil that cannot be ridden from society.

Persuasion, as a process, can be put into play by

closely analyzing the principal behavior exhibited by an individual and their subsequent response(s) during the course of an interaction. In this vein, persuasion can be deduced by the method of differentiating interaction from its relative responses. Hence, persuasion can be said to revolve around manipulating the cycle of cause and effect.

The Steps of Persuasion

During the process of being persuaded, analysis has shown a series of steps that the persuader employs on the persuaded.

These steps are listed below:

1. Communication:

It cannot be overemphasized that no form of persuasion can indeed be made possible without communicative interaction, as it is the primary medium by which the persuasive information is delivered. As such, when the information is first introduced, the persuaded assimilates it, paying attention to details, decoding its meaning, critiquing its proofs, and juxtaposing it against alternative others.

The first step of persuasion is completed if the persuader's argument resonates logically and is considered foolproof by the persuaded. The persuaded must assume the position offered by the newfound knowledge long enough to be able to expound on or implement it. This, therefore, makes the communicative process of persuasion a medium of verbal conviction meant to indict a new behavioral pattern based on the new information. For instance, when one is introduced to the concept of global warming as a hazard posed by not recycling materials and the irregular disposal of non-biodegradable materials, the person, once convinced, is persuaded to recycle more and use eco-friendly materials.

2. Repetition:

Often, people fail to be persuaded owing to a variety of reasons, such as poor communicative persuasion and dogmatism, as examples. It is on this account that repetition serves to play a better alternative to a failed communicative persuasive process.

The repetitive process of persuasion involves retrying the communicative persuasion process over and over until desired results are achieved. While this might seem like a bothersome process, research has shown that constant repetition of particular information is likely to have an effect in the long run. Based on this, a school of thought argues that persuasion and education share a close relationship in their repetitive processes. They are of the opinion that their similarity lies in the effective communication of new knowledge. And, as it is in education, repetition is employed over time as a means of modifying the learning process. This also applies to repetitive persuasion as persuaders seek to constantly improve on the premise of what they offer, bolstering its aesthetic and logical appeal so as to capture the persuaded.

The repetitive process of persuasion revolves around three key features, which are: Comprehension, retention, and attention. These features constitute the effect of the repetitive process on the persuaded, making sure the information is absorbed and retained. As an example, in business, advertisements are likely to be broadcasted repeatedly so as to influence the willpower of potential customers towards the goods or services offered.

3. Perception:

For persuasion to make its mark on the persuaded, the information passed must be able to resonate with the perception of the persuaded. In essence, the persuaded must be able to perceive the information as logical, foolproof, and worthy of indulgence; the image portrayed by the information has to appeal to the perceptive consciousness of the persuaded, because otherwise, the persuaded might feel defrauded and hard done by, subsequently cutting ties with the information and influencing others to rebuff it, too. Thusly, the response of the persuaded to the communicative process of persuasion leans heavily on the nature and appeal of the information as well as the meaning the persuaded derives from it.

Different information has distinct persuasiveness traits, as does the medium via which they are transmitted. For instance, an advert in a newspaper has a different persuasive content from an advertisement broadcasted on TV. The former is communicated through a written medium and is meant to be decoded by the persuaded. The latter, however, is communicated through spoken words and animated visuals that serve to relay to the persuaded their information. Juxtaposing both means that there is no direct telling to the audience they reach, but the authenticity of delivery is attained by the TV advert because it is aimed at appealing outright, while the newspaper advert is subject to the interpretation of the persuaded.

Another factor that constitutes persuasiveness is color. Colors are a vibration of light in varying degrees, hence they differ in their effect on people. Using colors can be a great way to influence the perception of the persuaded. For instance, the colors red, orange, and yellow have been associated with hunger, cravings, and a quest to satiate. Organizations that offer food services to the public seize this color advantage, using them in their designs and décor, appealing to the perception of the hungry and persuading them to try their menus.

In general, perceptual persuasion revolves around changing or influencing an individual's cognition of a particular behavioral pattern. A perceptual approach to persuasion requires that cognizance is given to the opinions of the persuaded and adequate proof is provided to support the communicated information. This denotes that the behavior of the persuaded is understood and the persuasive effort made aligns to quell any inhibition and to influence a change. This step, unlike the previous (repetition), prioritizes comprehension and attention alone.

4. Situations:

Situational persuasion seizes the advantage of the present environment to make its mark. It employs the technique of preying on conditions that would otherwise yield little to no result at other times. Hence, situational persuasion is a time-relative persuasive step. And, it is no lie that its time-factor quality inferences its merits and demerits.

Situational persuasion seeks to exploit the cognitive, physical, and emotional conditions of its target audience during communicating, so as to influence willpower. It is by this means the persuader is likely to meet the audience's needs or to convince them into being patronized. For instance, the theory of crowd power has shown that persuasion is more likely to be effective among a crowd of people than individually with the exact same people. This argument stems from Gustave Le Bon, who observed that the behavioral patterns of people differ if they are considered as a group or as a single entity. Le Bon is of the opinion that a single individual is stronger cognitively than a crowd of people. Of course, this condition only applies according to the size of the crowd and its measure of willingness. Drawing situational persuasion into this instance, a group of people is more likely to be persuaded than an individual is, but sometimes the reverse could also be the case. However, persuasive success begins with a member of the crowd being convinced. Next, the conviction travels virally through other members who might also be convinced, until finally, it reaches the remainder who, against their better judgments, do not want to be the sore thumb in the crowd. The final set of people noted in this instance have their individual abilities to resist persuasion rendered incapable by the homogeneity of the crowd, which also reduces the prominence of their distinct behaviors and their sense of self.

In another instance, say, during winter, people would require less persuasion to be convinced into buying goods and services to help protect themselves against the cold. This instance serves situational persuasion in being able to meet its required targets by exploiting their needs in alignment with the weather conditions.

How to Influence People

The world today thrives on being able to influence the populace towards a particular point and keeping them long enough to have the desired effect. This is seen daily in the activities of business, politics, social interactions, education, religion, and even personal conviction. The aforementioned all seek to persuade people with their distinct ideologies, biding their time to be able to manipulate the willpower, cognition, emotion, or sense of self of their target audiences. However, one thing is common to them all—influence. Each influencer wishes to attain control over their audience and effect a change beneficial to themselves. And, while this may sound outright outrageous and exploitive, it is the system the world operates in, both collectively and individually. It is by this means that organization is maintained and order is kept, without making people seem like they are being made pawns of. Hence, it is arguably factual to concede that the world revolves around influence.

This proves that human beings have a measure of their behavior subject to external influences, which, mutually, interacts and influences—and can be influenced itself—by our choices.

Influence could come in both positive and negative shades, with each bearing its peculiarities, however, they both trigger the cycle of cause and effect, resulting in responses in either vein. On this account, a positive form of influence is likely to result in more positive results, while the negative form of influence is likely to result in more tragic responses. And, although persuasion can be accounted for as a means of influencing people, there exist many other different ways of manipulating people towards a cause.

These are considered as follows:

1. Fear:

There is not one human treading the earth without a bit of fear in their essence. Fear, in itself, forms the building blocks upon which character is built or marred. Fear could arguably pass for the strongest emotion in human perception, owing to its complicated and often misjudged nature, and its relative measure in every person. The complicated nature of fear arises from its ability to assume both positive and negative fronts and be used to influence changes on either side. That is, fear isn't necessarily an evil emotion as it also has its good sides, which, when subjected to ample control and judicious use, is capable of spurring an individual to great heights. Albeit, fear is commonly known for the unpleasant, inhibitive, and damage-ridden trail it leaves in its wake when put to negative use.

Such negative use is common in present-day society where it is wielded by leaders to influence the people into submission. Here, fear is applied amply to affect or control the cognition, actions, and emotions of the people by means of biased societal ideologies, mass media, education, communication, and passive aggression. Also, leaders of past ages who ruled in despotism understood human behavior enough to be able to invoke the impact fear causes, thus manipulating the populace into doing their bidding.

On the other hand, the relative measure of fear, in the essence of human behavior, evolves with the primary characteristics of a person as a means of adaptation, meant to be a defensive mechanism to assure successive survival, albeit fear in modern times has evolved with civilization and human adaptation into very distinct forms. These forms account for caveats in human behavior that make an individual capable of being influenced.

For instance, in contemporary times, fear has progressed into phobias, taking on diverse unfounded forms with no tangible meanings, yet seemingly affecting human psychology.

Besides phobias, many other fears derive from psychological and cognitive origins, such as a fear of death, the unknown, a fear of failure, of losing, damnation, rejection (especially in love or ambition), and pain. These fears account for the surest means by which an individual can be influenced and, once the individual's fear is triggered, the cycle of cause and effect kicks in to bring about an influenced response of fight or flight i.e. once a person's fear is incited, they can be manipulated into facing this fear (fight) or cowering from it (flight).

For instance, theists lacking in piety are more

likely to be influenced into being more reverential by the fear of damnation than their atheist counterparts. This stems from theists dreading the punishment held by their beliefs on account of abandonment of duty, while atheists have no beliefs and, therefore, no fear of punishment. This purely denotes that a theist is influenced into subjective duty by the fear that their belief holds over them.

In conclusion, research has revealed that fear is just as dominant across the ages as much as love is. This is backed up by proof of fear as a natural entity common to all—the pious and the impious, the political and the apolitical, the leader and the slave; in short: Mankind. As such, everyone is capable of experiencing fear and being feared, making fear more universally dominant than love. Niccolò Machiavelli captures this dominance in his theories where he questioned if it was preferable to be feared rather than. He argued that it would be the utmost option to be feared and loved all at once, but since both phenomena are simply immiscible, one has to make do with either. He conceded that being loved comes with an even greater price of little to no security than being feared. And, since love's endurance is an entity that binds man to his fellow man, it is easily subject to being broken whenever it inhibits a selfish advantage. On the other hand, he conceded that fear is an undying phenomenon with physical evidence of pain, which is terrifying. Thus, the only power over fear is a much greater fear.

2. Nudges:

When human behavior is incapable of being influenced by fear, nudges sometimes serve as a more subtle means. To nudge indicates a gentle push, meant to gain the attention of an individual and influence them down a particular path. This action acts as a signal used to assert persuasive techniques on an individual.

Nudges represent the decisive alterations made during the course of persuasive communication as a means of influencing human behavior. These decisive alterations arise from the measure of predictability expressed by the influenced. Nudges, unlike fear, present a much humane way of altering the behavior and choices of people, without the need of personal and societal influences such as beliefs, interests, and culture. But, very much like fear, nudges can be employed by anyone, with an aim to influence the choices and behavioral patterns of people towards a target goal or path.

One great quality of nudges that sets them apart from other means of influential behavior is its ability to be used on oneself for personal gain. For example, when attempt individuals trying to bereave themselves of the unending craving for chocolate, they are likely to be more successful by nudging. First, the individual is required to keep chocolates from sight; literally above eye level and out of vision range. Once this feat is attained, all that is left is for these individuals to constantly nudge themselves towards eating healthier foods as alternatives for their chocolate craving.

Nudges come in a variety of forms, each dependent on the target audience and goal. Examples include: Religious nudges meant to groom the faithful, societal nudges meant to keep organized, and personal nudges, as in the example above, to meet certain goals. Like all factors of influence, nudges maintain neutrality and can be put to either positive or negative use.

Nudges also exist as two main types: Mindful and mindless.

Mindful nudges refer to the conscious efforts put into influencing the choices and behavior of individuals. Simply put, mindful nudges are the means employed in influencing people by making them aware of the aftereffects of their choices and behaviors. It offers an individual a chance to pump the brakes on rash decisions, opting instead for carefully reconsidered alternatives. Mindful nudges are a necessary part of daily living because they provide people with the extra edge required to go through the hustle and bustle of each day successfully when they otherwise would have rushed through it all leaving behind strings of poor choices in their trail.

Mindless nudges, on the other hand, denote less avid efforts put into influencing human behavior and choices beyond the perceptive consciousness. In other words, unlike mindful nudges, mindless nudges uses unconscious means of influencing an individual. This denotes that a person's behavior could be changed with no consciously perceivable clue given to the person. Mindless nudges play out as subtle, ingenious alterations made in the presentation of persuasive information that influences the subconscious and subsequent choices and behaviors. Owing to its preference for a more unobvious approach, mindless nudges affect people without their knowledge.

3. **Beliefs:**

Beliefs play a significant role in our lives, accounting also for behavioral patterns. Whether in the absence or presence of belief in a particular phenomenon, people are highly likely to be influenced in a given way if the mode of influence resonates with the rationality of their beliefs; consider beliefs as a second cognitive process by which people are likely to base their choices or behaviors off of.

For example, terrorist groups are fond of sending their members into oblivion with very weak promises. These members are sent to engage in tasks that are otherwise considered insane by those of different beliefs. However, these members still perform these tasks without fear, which would mark their imminent deaths. This is only possible because their belief of a place in paradise as a reward for their deeds blinds them to the pain and insanity of their actions. This instance shows just how much the belief system of an individual, sometimes independent of logic and sentiment, influences them.

Belief, in this sense, can be deduced to mean the reception of a phenomenon as true regardless of whether or not there is tangible evidence to support its existence. It could also mean a system of faith and trust built upon a person or thing considered to be true in individualistic perspectives. Belief arguably rivals fear in dominance as an influential factor if it doesn't exactly trump it. This, of course, is on account that beliefs have been around for as long as our ability to comprehend, adapt, and interact with the environment, and the fact that it employs fear, nudges, and willpower in influencing behavior. As such, beliefs account for an important factor responsible for creating, controlling, and influencing the human behavioral patterns.

Manipulating the Power and Freedom of Will (Willpower and Free Will)

Although willpower and free will maybe appear to be one and the same, they are very different, with distinct individual meanings.

Willpower refers to the resolute intensity of the will needed to execute a person's desire(s). It indicates the decisive, effectual power of intent in attaining a given longing. Free will, on the other hand, indicates the natural, unimposed desires of a person; simply put, it is the freedom an individual exhibits in determining their choices, actions, and overall behavior. This freedom is independent of the restrictions posed by influence, predestination, necessity, and fate; the individual is left to their devices and discretion. Homogeneously, willpower and free will denote a psychological or mental freedom of unrestrained intent.

Willpower and free will go a long way in interpreting a person and providing insights into the products of their choices and actions. And, while this portrays these phenomena as being major caveats to be exploited in trying to manipulate human behavior, they fall short by how they are being put to use. This is on account of the fact that a good many people fail to exercise their willpower and free will in contemporary times owing to the societal, religious, cultural, and personal influences that are almost always higher placed than them. This is not necessarily bad news, because unused willpower or free will offers another perspective to be manipulated of; thus, the failure to harness the power and freedom of will is a much better alternative than a misunderstanding and misuse of will.

Manipulating the will of people involves the subtle process of exploiting the power of the primary factors that influence their lives. These factors of influence, which include culture, fears, beliefs, personal perceptions, and desires, provide the loophole by which people can be psychologically manipulated into submission. This is proven by history itself, having a record of leaders who have employed the trick of manipulating the power and freedom of wills to their advantage. History portrays these leaders to have procured absolute power over people by simply limiting the power and freedom the people have over their wills. In essence, these leaders bereaved the people of the right to choose and judge freely by abolishing all options, leaving the people incapable of personal judgments or opinions. As such, the people were subjected to a particular mode of behavior by reason of their inability to determine anything.

Another technique of manipulating the power and freedom of will is in allowing people to a selected range of choices. Here, their freedom of choice and judgment is not taken away but leashed. The people are conditioned into believing that restricting their right to choice and judgment is not the same as, and is a more preferable an option to, an outright abolishment of this right. This then highlights their vulnerability of being influenced by conditions towards the more suitable which isn't necessarily ideal in itself.

This technique gives people the feeling of being a

part of the decision process, like they are in charge of their choices when actually they aren't. As a matter of fact, the people are being made pawns by the manipulators who stand to achieve their goals, regardless of the choices the people make from the options available. For instance, imagine these scenarios: A rock and a hard place, and the devil and the deep blue sea. Neither indicates a safer way out as an option, but people would rather have two options than one or none at all. Somehow, they are placated by the understanding that one of the options in each scenario is better than the other. Simply put, the ideology of a lesser evil seems to them to hold a better appeal, however, this is not the case, as the manipulator has them stuck in a maze of riddles with neither of the options being the correct one to let them out.

The Art of Subtle Manipulations

Manipulating the will of people is one thing, but keeping them manipulated long enough to achieve a target is another. It is in man's nature to be rebellious and question systems over time. As such, for a manipulative process to be considered successful, the manipulated must remain a pawn, and a pawn is never in the know of its stance. To subtly manage a manipulation, the manipulated must be seduced into agreeing with the target plan. The seductive process is, of course, persuasive communication dedicated to influencing the behavior of the manipulated. This is only possible by preying on the vulnerability of their psychology and behavioral system and is the making of a faithful pawn.

As mentioned earlier about the rebellion's nature of man, times would come when even the most faithful pawn would query the manipulator. In this case, it is left to the latter to put to test this uprising through manipulative means.

The resistant front of the manipulated can be quelled via a host of means:

- Guilt-tripping them into believing they are

ungrateful.

- Exploiting their emotions by playing the victim.

- Using controlled anger.

- Use their belief systems against them.

- Engaging in conditional persuasions.

- Employing their virtues as caveats to manipulate their actions.

- Be charming, shallowly sympathetic and flattering.

Chapter 3: Using the Knowledge of Human Psychology to Your Advantage (Tips and Tricks)

To successfully be able to manipulate a person's psychology and get them to act in your favor, you must first have an understanding of why they behave the way they do. It is a fact that no two people are exactly alike in any aspect. From the differences in our DNA to the unique ways our minds perceive the various societies in which we grow up, it is obvious as to why our thoughts are as distinct as the prints on our fingers. This is easily noticeable during arguments; when two people argue, it is often not because they have differing opinions. Sometimes, if you listen well enough, the problem is in the way they express their similar views on a topic. You may notice that even though these individuals are debating for the same sides, they are still arguing. One beauty of psychology is that people have a defined image of themselves and they try to live up to it. We reveal the nature of our psyche by the things we say, our choice of words, the type of clothes we prefer, the nature of our spending, how we react to a crisis, who we vote for and why, etc.

If you would like to take advantage of these characteristics of human behavior, the prerequisites are observance and knowledge. Below are a few situations that may demand the application of some psychology hacks in order to turn the tables in your favor.

- Think of a time in your life when you really wished you could avoid the full blast of someone's anger. This may be your boss, parents or relationship partner, whose outbursts always leave you with a pit in your stomach or just praying the ground beneath your feet would swallow you whole. All you needed to do was be in close proximity to that person and you would have, to a large extent, extinguished their ire. How easy would you say it is to lash out at someone who is seated right next to you? Awkward at best, don't you think? This is, partly, because we have a tendency to raise our voices when we are upset. As a result, you, unconsciously, would prefer some distance between you and whoever you are venting at. Once you have succeeded at pacifying anyone by sitting or standing close to them, you may then go on to make a case in your favor and win them over. Practice this tip if, at any point, you find yourself at the uncomfortable end of anyone's wrath.

- Be careful with how you reward people for completing a task. Human beings are prone to developing a sense of entitlement and may get lost in that illusion. You may only be doing this with the best of intentions and to boost their productivity, but, goodwill or not, this has the potential of backfiring. People need to feel driven to perform a task of any kind for the sake of it alone. They should feel joy and passion for the job as the major encouragement for going through with it every time. You may think that a special reward would get this done, but it could defeat the entire purpose. Besides the fact that a few individuals may start feeling overly deserving, others around you may feel like they have failed in their tasks and, as a consequence, might experience a decrease in their level of self-confidence. Healthy competition is good, but it should be engaged in just because. People should compete, without strife, merely for the sake of growth and development of self. This reward system is not entirely a bad thing. If done sparingly, it truly could increase productivity.

- Get cognitive dissonance to work for you. You will notice, even with your own self, that a person is more at peace when their thoughts concerning a thing are in tandem with their actions towards it. Your mind, reflexively, rebels against cognitive dissonance, which is knowledge that you should put to use in getting people to like you. To do this, you should get people to do you a favor with no expected reward. If you can successfully accomplish this, the person in question would have a redefined image of you in their mind. After all, you can't be so bad a human being if they just helped you out. Cognitive dissonance is also factored by repetition. When we form a habit of behaving in any particular way, there is usually the tendency of us continuing in that set pattern. It requires less thought to simply react as usual than to change and decide on a new course of action towards that thing. If you have established a history of dishing out good advice, people may not bother to vet your future advice or disagreements after a while.

- Remember how Dracula could literally control a person by looking them in the eye? Well, maybe that concept is not entirely fictional. You don't have to stare at people till it's creepy and uncomfortable. The key here is to maintain eye contact when meeting someone for the first time. Whether or not you are naturally a shy and introverted person, this is not information they need to have on the first meeting. As you shake their hand and introduce yourself, do not fall into the habit of looking away at the floor, or anywhere else, except who you are speaking with. This portrays a lack of self-confidence and puts a serious dent in whatever charm you were hoping to exude. Look your speaking companion in the eye and maintain it for a few heartbeats before breaking contact. It would also bolster your confidence and help you find your voice.

- During interviews, you don't have to feel backed into a tight corner and like a threatened rabbit. You would be asked a slew of questions, some of which you know very well but refuse to be processed from your brain and out your mouth because of unsteady nerves. A way to calm yourself and create a good image in the mind of your interviewer is to ask them questions in turn. These questions should not be politically incorrect, assuming, flirtatious or rude. You may start by saying you feel a little nervous but cannot wait to be one of their employees. Then you could ask when they started working there and what their experience has been like. Simply getting them to talk about themselves would go a long way into breaking the barrier between you and the interviewer, and leave them a favorable and distinct impression of you.

- With the help of psychology as a

discipline, we are now aware of how to have someone help us out with things they would otherwise have declined. No, you don't have to pressure anyone, blackmail them or play on their feelings of guilt in order to have your way. The simple method to accomplish this is to first propose something of a larger magnitude. Say you would like a friend to fix breakfast, lunch or dinner. They are more likely to do it if you ask them instead to go out and buy groceries (this would be more effective if the friend has a dislike for grocery shopping). This psychology tip functions on the premise that people are not very likely to refuse you more than once. Should you then ask the friend to cook after they have declined to shop for groceries, chances are that they would say yes.

- This tip may seem weird, but it works so well. We cannot even bother to question its means. What method does it use to manipulate a person's psychology, you ask? All you would have to do is mirror the actions of the other person. Cool stuff, wouldn't you say? It is called pacing, and I know this may not seem like a very fitting name but that's beside the point. By copying the body language and speech pattern of the conversation partner, you put them at ease and can more easily convince them to do what you wanted of them. That said, this may require a little bit of practice before you try it in a real-life situation. You sure don't want to come off as strange to your boss or whoever you are speaking with. With pacing, you have to be conscious of how the person in front of you moves their feet, their gesticulations, eye movements, and the subtle (or not so subtle) changes in their intonations. All these should be mirrored back to them without ever being obvious. Regardless of how this may seem to you, I suggest you give it a try. Read up on it, practice with a control situation and see how it goes.

- Take the time observe and take mental notes of the person whose psychology you would like to control. Some of this has already been mentioned in earlier paragraphs but will be mentioned in more detail for further emphasis. As a result of the differing qualities that separate one person from another, some study should be conducted before you apply any psychology tips to manipulate them. This shouldn't take too long a time before you can come to a conclusion as to the most effective way to go about it. Things like temperaments and personality types should be given due consideration as it would go a long way in determining which approach would produce the best results. You don't want to attempt playing to a person's empathy when they find it easy to detach themselves from such emotions.

Others may not be so rational and would more easily be swayed by a spur of the moment requests. This observational study would save you from some really embarrassing moments and isn't a lot of work when compared to the results you are likely to see. Take notice of the little things that would naturally go over your head and decide on the best way to get that person to give in to your requests.

- Be very logical and cover all your bases. This is something you may already do without knowing it, but it would be more effective if you did it intentionally. Before asking anything of anyone, consider all the probable excuses they might pose in order to get out of giving in to you. Find the perfect argument to defeat those excuses and successfully disarm them. You may even show them the ways, if they exist, in which they could benefit from helping you out. This tip would work really well if you also apply the previous point about observing people. You would have a more rounded knowledge of what you have gotten into and why you should keep total control throughout the entire conversation. Although, how you react in any situation depends largely on how important the goal is to you, but if you put any thought and work into making this tip work, the results may just prove truly satisfying. Have it all planned out to make your point seem like the only reasonable stance, without seeming too insistent.

- Go glass half full on them. Turn the perspective a full 360 so that their initial argument doesn't hold water anymore, even in their own eyes. You may even agree with the counter-arguments before pointing out the flaws that they contain. Talk about how going your way instead would be more beneficial and explain in which ways this can be made possible. You should do this without making the person you are trying to convince look silly or intellectually lazy, though. Only show, possibly with proof, that your idea is the more profitable one with the view of making them dump or shelf theirs. In other words, the goal of your argument should make them doubt their own argument and not themselves.

Chapter 4 : The Driving Force of Human Behavior (Motivation)

Whether it is the involuntary response to stimuli or a decisive response during an interaction, all human behavior arises as a result of a driving force. The scientist, Isaac Newton noted in his theories of motion that there is no reaction (response) without a causal action (driving force). In psychology, this opinion is expressed in human behavior as the cycle of cause and effect. As such, all effects (responses) stem from causes, which are the primary driving forces.

These driving forces of human behavior are categorized under the term, 'motivation.' This is on account of the reason that any other phenomena considered pivotal in influencing human behavior has a target goal, which inevitably makes it a motive. And, since all behavioral patterns, be it voluntary or involuntary, are aimed at particular endpoints, they are motivation-based.

What, then, is motivation?

Motivation refers to the forces of cognition, emotion, society, and biology being jointly responsible for a particular behavioral pattern. In other words, motivation can be seen as the cognitive and emotional processes that trigger, maintain, and influence actions interpreted as behavior.

That is, Cognition + Emotion = Actions (behavior).

These actions are always objective-oriented because no behavior is without purpose or cause. In essence, motivation is what propels an individual. For instance, in eating, the action is propelled by the need to sate hunger. Hence, the motivation here is the hunger. Another instance is in prepping for an exam: The propelling force is the need to pass, thus the motivation, in this case, is the desire to not fail.

Motives denote the purpose of human behavior. They concede the most innate, basic reasons that result in a specific behavioral pattern, highlighting the response as sprouts stemming off of them. Motives, in their real states, cannot be observed, what with the fact that they are abstract processes of cognition and emotions. However, motives can be deduced from the corresponding action that is birthed of the cognitive and emotional processes. Simply put, the corresponding action—interpreted as the behavior—is what is capable of being traced back to the motive.

The Driving Factors of Motives

Motives might control behavior, but they are not, themselves, totally independent from control. Psychologists of human behavior are of the opinion that certain factors control or influence motives. These factors are inclusive but not limited to biology, cognition, emotions, culture, beliefs, and society, among others. All these factors, individually or collectively, constitute to the formation of a motive, thus earning their place as the innate drivers of human behavior.

However, other schools of thought have, over time, argued for some factors being of higher importance and value in driving motives and should thus be given more prominence. Three factors emerged as the key driving forces of motives and are postulated in distinct theories suggesting how they most influence motives:

1. The Theory of Drives (Needs):

The theory of drives is based on the natural conditioning of the body towards satisfaction. It denotes the biological inclination of an individual towards certain needs as the primary reason of behavior, which is in itself a motivated response towards satisfying such needs. Simply put, this theory indicates the biological drives that account for the motives behind human behavior.

For instance, itchiness, hunger, and exhaustion are all biologically inclined drives that propel different responses from an individual. The individual, on account of biological influence, is propelled to satisfy these needs by itching, eating, and sleeping, respectively. That is, a biological need for scratching, sleep, and food motivated the individual into scratching, sleeping, and eating.

2. The Theory of Instincts:

The theory of instincts arises from the responses of humans, especially when based on a process of thoughts of no conscious or rational origins. This theory indicates that human behavior is born of impulses. The school of thought proposing this theory concede that human behavior is motivated by the innate, unchangeable patterns that make up behavior—instincts.

Instincts, owing to their abstract nature, are only perceivable by biological and cognitive sensitization. And, although instincts can be sensed on account of many different reasons, they constitute a huge part of the behavioral patterns of humans. Instincts hold such deep grounds in the motivation of behavior because they cut across both the voluntary and involuntary responses of people to varying circumstances.

For instance, instincts are responsible for the action of fight or flight (response) when danger is spotted. This response could be either voluntary or involuntary. Another example would be the withdrawal from a hot object; the response, in this case, is involuntary because the action of recoiling wasn't on the basis of careful thoughts.

Instincts earmark the response of people as motivated by biological inclinations towards satisfying specific needs. Biologically inclined instincts include love, fear, defense, cleanliness, stimuli, and basically every other phenomenon important to the successive adaptation and survival of a person.

Psychologists who are also of the opinion that primary biological drives influence overall human behavior include William McDougal, William James, and Sigmund Freud.

3. The Theory of Arousal:

The theory of arousal borders on the stimulation of feelings as the motivation that propels behavior. It focuses on the biological nature of human beings to be stimulated and respond in like regards to their feelings.

The theory of arousal is of the opinion that human behavior is an adaptive process resulting from persons being motivated towards maintaining a balance in their arousal states until an ideal arousal level is attained. This theory aligns with the concept of personality types popularized by the psychologist, Carl Jung. The psychologist, Hans Eysenck, conceded in his theories that arousal levels differ across a single continuum. Eysenck opined that 15% of people possessed low levels of arousal, another 15% possessed much higher arousal levels, and a concluding 70% laid in the middle. This theory indicates that the 15% with lower arousal levels are extroverts, explaining why they are easily motivated to indulge in thrilling, exciting, and louder experiences so as to meet an ideal arousal level. The second 15%, on the other hand, are introverts who naturally possess much higher arousal levels, which accounts for why introverts pursue quieter, smaller, and less rigorous indulgences as a means of escaping overstimulation. This makes them able to keep their rather high arousal levels optimal. The final 70%, since they are in between, have both introversive and extroversive qualities, and take on both characteristics distinctly as a means of straining balance in arousal levels.

In all, every individual possesses a level of arousal particular to them. This stems from biological factors like personality inclination, adaptation, and environment, which when combined, constitute the levels of arousal an individual is short of—or above—on the optimal arousal scale. In this vein, people are likely to seek stimulating activities to increase their arousal levels and relaxing activities to curb overstimulation. In essence, this theory indicates that human behavior is forged by the motivated pursuit of stimulating activities in order to attain balance and optimal arousal levels.

Classification of Motivation

As can be deduced from the aforementioned theories, motivation arises on account of many biological factors. These factors cut across vast psychological fronts and would make for an endless list, if not classified. Hence, these factors are classified into 2 categories, based on the similarities they share in how an individual perceives them distinctly: Intrinsic and extrinsic motivation.

Intrinsic Motivation

Intrinsic motivation refers to any propelling force that influences an individual into a particular behavior. In intrinsic motivation, there is no external influence motivating the individual towards a behavioral pattern; hence, the individual is indulgent of their own volition and urges. For example, if an individual habitually engages in trying out the game of Sudoku on the back page of every newspaper he or she buys, they engage in this activity for the personal gains of doing some brain work, not necessarily because there is a prize to be won.

From this example, it is obvious that this individual expresses intrinsic behavior because he or she acts independently of the influence of an external benefit. Rather, the individual enjoys indulging in the activity, considering it a means of learning, bettering oneself, and exploring their potential—in essence, personal gains.

Pursuing activities solely for the purpose of enjoyment is motivated by intrinsic forces within an individual. These forces influence a particular behavior so as to attain internal satisfaction rather than external benefits. This doesn't necessarily connote that behaviors stemming from intrinsic motives don't have rewards particular to them. No, intrinsically motivated behaviors are rewarded by the internal feeling of satisfaction, happiness, having fun, and other such positive emotions. People are more likely to be intrinsically motivated towards activities if they feel inclined towards trying new things, learning and relearning, seeking accomplishments, grooming themselves, seeking meaning, and tracking progress. Here, intrinsic motivation influences them towards meeting these goals at their pace without feeling forced into it. Simply put, intrinsic motivation influences them into indulging voluntarily into activities and achieving decisively made goals.

Intrinsic motivation plays a major role in determining human behavior and response while performing certain activities. It portrays the primary behavior of people in a natural state of no-rewards and self-satisfaction. This condition makes intrinsic motivation an important and necessary addition to everyday life. For instance, if every duty ever assigned to everyone was performed by intrinsic motivation, there would be less half-hearted, disgruntled workers, which would mean better services and even better pay. Life could be more fun if every other thing was born of intrinsic motivation.

This instance shows just how much intrinsic motivation could contribute immensely to a given system. It is no wonder, then, why it is being adopted in the educational system now. Sadly, the education system isn't thoroughly driven by intrinsic motivation, so learners have had to be motivated by external benefits such as scholarships, fund schemes, students' loans, and academic prizes. This makes the process of learning more of a means to an end than an actually enjoyed, understood, and enthusiastically anticipated prospect. However, in recent times, educationists are striving to induce the process of learning under intrinsically motivating standards to help make the paradigm shift on how learning is viewed. This would help change the mindset of learning being boring and a chore that would otherwise require extrinsic motivation to be indulged in.

Study has shown that intrinsic motivation is the cheapest and most satisfying form of influence since it comes at no unprecedented price, influences an individual towards a well-liked, voluntary path, and constitutes a properly balanced life. It also concedes that people's performance, will, interest, and motivation is not inevitably influenced by external benefits.

Factors That Influence Intrinsic Motivation

Although intrinsic motivation is inherent and, thus, isn't born of forces outside people, it is promoted by certain factors, inclusive but not limited to the following:

I. Recognition:

Recognition is the condition of being considered

valid, valuable, and befitting of notice. It is an inherent quality in our nature to crave a measure of attention. Intrinsic motivation is likely to increase when the performance and feats of people receive a reasonable amount of recognition due. This, in itself, acts as a propellant to further influence the person towards being better. An example of this are the people who are awarded for the giant strides they have made in any particular field or their sacrifices towards a safer and better society. This serves to encourage them into doing even more of what they had been doing by recognize this effort and the effects it has had.

II. Challenges:

Challenges refers to tasks of varying difficulties that are attempted by people who find their experience rather enjoyable. Challenges prove to be a key method of motivating people into attempting a pursuit of targets that they find meaningful and satisfactory to them, as individuals. Challenges are embarked on because the targets are considered attainable and not inevitably certain. They offer attainable goals of significance to a person and provides a means of bettering oneself and learning.

III. Competition and Cooperation:

Cooperation refers to any form of association that results in mutuality of benefits. Competition, on the other hand, refers to contesting under similar rules, standards, and events. People are likely to be motivated intrinsically when satisfaction is mutual with others. That is, in cases where one is satisfied by helping another, the former is propelled towards such activity continuously. In another case of competition, people are motivated towards improving or continuing on a streak when they are able to successively juxtapose their abilities against others.'

IV. Curiosity:

Curiosity indicates the probability of a person to inquire into a phenomenon by means of investigation, inquiry, and exploration. The essence of curiosity borders on the condition of a phenomenon being interesting and able to capture attention. Since it is natural for man to be drawn towards the attractive and unusual, intrinsic motivation propels one towards curiosity.

As such, intrinsic motivation could be on account of curiosity. Intrinsic motivation can be triggered by two types of curiosity: Sensory and cognitive. The former makes for an increase in intrinsic motivation when an individual is drawn to a phenomenon perceivable in the physical consciousness. The latter, however, occurs when the indulgence in an activity motivates an individual into craving knowledge of it via learning.

V.   **Control:**

To control means the ability to assume influence over a thing, making one capable of determining subsequent choices and behavior. The desire to be in charge of one's environment and self proves to be an overwhelming influence on intrinsic characteristics. We have often sought the ability to determine our pursuits and choices, with the motivation to venture down this path coming from within.

Extrinsic Motivation

The term 'extrinsic' indicates anything of external origin that is independent of another thing, usually a host. In relation to immediate motivation, extrinsic motivation indicates any form of influence not inherent in an individual but responsible for certain behaviors in the individual. Unlike its alternative other, intrinsic motivation, extrinsic motivation stems from external factors that prompt specific patterns of behavior in an individual. Since the factors of extrinsic behavior are outside of a person, the subsequent reward of the action (behavior) is also external. Examples of these external rewards can be recognition, monetary rewards, praise, trophies, grades, and fame, as examples.

In extrinsic motivation, these external rewards are the main motivators that drive the individual's behavior, causing them to assume a particular pattern of behavior in order to achieve them. For instance, a student studying for a scholarship exam and another student reading leisurely both have diverse reading intensities and motives. The former is motivated (extrinsically) by the scholarship (external reward) to study harder. The latter, on the other hand, engages in reading as an enjoyed experience and is motivated (intrinsically) towards the activity because of the satisfaction (internal reward) derived from it.

Extrinsic motivation, however, has its downside in being the sole reason for why an individual could express a particular behavior, even though the individual would otherwise behave differently if there weren't any external rewards involved. That is, unlike intrinsic motivation in which people are propelled towards behaviors they enjoy and do willingly, people are less likely to be extrinsically motivated to a task in which they stand to gain nothing. Extrinsically motivated individuals would continue in a particular behavioral pattern even when they feel no personal attraction or likeness for and towards it.

To buttress this point, an instance is taken of everyday workers. A good many workers hate what they do as a job, feel they aren't being given enough credit, and are, on the whole, disillusioned by their jobs. However, these workers continue in these jobs because they are extrinsically motivated by their paychecks. In essence, their continued commitment is not necessarily out of love or passion but for the monthly, weekly or fortnightly paycheck they are given. Thus, extrinsic motivation thrives as external rewards last.

Extrinsic Motivation and Reward Types

Since extrinsic motivation borders on the likelihood of an individual performing an activity on account of an agreed, external prize, it is important that cognizance is given to the types of reward it offers and how it affects the individual. The rewards that prompt extrinsic motivation are of two categories: Psychological and tangible rewards.

1. **Psychological Rewards:**

Psychological rewards refer to those intangible rewards that promote extrinsic motivation. They are considered intangible because they are not physically perceptible but have an effect on the psychology of an individual and is capable of motivating them towards a behavioral pattern. Some examples of psychological rewards include recognition, fame, and praise.

As an example, children are likely to maintain 'good' behavior when their little good deeds are recognized and praised by their parents. Also, musicians, asides the awards they vie for, seek to be their best in order to attain fame. The same is also the case with movie makers, who give their all to their art in order to capture the hearts of viewers and receive praise and worldwide acclaim. One common factor in all these examples is the fact that an unphysical, intangible reward motivates these persons towards behaving in a certain manner. And, while it might seem that this type of extrinsic reward might hold intrinsic qualities of self-satisfaction, the pursued goal and motivator is from external means, thus, it is an extrinsic motivation.

2. Tangible Rewards:

Tangible rewards are ones that are perceptible to the physical senses; that is, they are able to be seen, touched, and felt. This type of reward is common in the educational sector, business, and politics, as examples. Tangible rewards are used to set certain standards that must be met in order to achieve the rewards. In striving to meet these standards, people are indirectly being motivated by the prize towards a particular behavior.

For instance, in teaching a dog new tricks, if one decidedly gives the dog a treat for every time the dog does a trick correctly, the dog is likely to behave accordingly in order to gain the treat. Another example being cyclists enduring weather conditions, jet lag, and exhaustion in order to come out top in a race and receive a reward; while contesting for this reward, the cyclists are made to adapt to strenuous conditions they wouldn't otherwise go through willingly. This represents just how the reward motivates an enduring behavior in the cyclists.

Overall, extrinsic motivation is as effective as the availability of an external reward and the willingness of individuals. However, research has shown that continued extrinsic motivation could necessitate a decrease in intrinsic motivation. A continued decline of the latter would mean a continuous need for extrinsic motivation, which would prove rather expensive to manage.

Chapter 5: Human Behavior and Irrationality

Irrationality refers to any cognitive process of speaking, acting and thinking bereft of the idealism of rationality. In essence, irrationality is used to depict any perspective of thought or action considered to be below par to philosophical idealism, proper cognitive functionality or emotional wellbeing. In everyday life, irrationality is considered disparagingly to mean a pattern of actions and thoughts that are unsound, useless, and of no relation to its alternative other—rationality.

In relation to behavior, irrationality denotes a behavioral pattern that isn't influenced by logic, cognition or reason. Irrational behavior indicates actions and opinions, which are born of a thought process not thoroughly thought out. As such, the driving force of irrational behavior is almost incapable of being understood even though the behavior is aimed at meeting a target.

Irrationality in behavior could be a behavioral disorder in an individual from which they can snap out from or one that requires medical aid. Irrational behavior can occur in people on account of a host of factors, like anxiety, overthinking, and phobias, as examples, propelling them towards actions that seem to fulfill their needs but, by rational standards, are rather absurd. Some examples of irrational behaviors in people include: Behaving irresponsibly for absolutely no reason, being mad at a future situation, and exaggerated expressions of feelings. In all these examples, the people involved aren't exactly in the wrong for their expressions, however, the timing, patterns, and motives for each behavior makes their expressions seem far from rational standards.

Another example could be including a knock-knock coffin joke in a funeral eulogy; it wouldn't exactly account as being the best of rational behaviors. This is because, while the joke isn't necessarily bad in itself, it is ill-timed and not befitting of the rationale of the situation. This makes the listening audience consider the speaker irrational, not on account of his appearance or fluency, but the decision to aberrate.

Of all the types of behavior, irrational behavior stands out as one having no defined target or meaning. As is deducible from the example above, the purpose of including a joke in a eulogy isn't clearly thought out, and the motive doesn't exactly qualify as being 'right.' This portrays irrationality as a behavior that seems right to an individual on impulse but, once exhibited, becomes meaningless.

Studies show that irrationality is an embodiment of human nature characterized by impulsive actions that are given no conclusive thoughts. In essence, it describes the way people behave without considering the outcome of their behaviors.

For example, cyclists know driving without their

safety gear is a risky endeavor, yet, not a day goes by without people blitzing by without helmets. They do not do it on account of ignorance, but, on the contrary, they know it's dangerous to be unprotected against accidents but they do it all the same. They don't think of the unforeseen contingencies that might arise from their actions, or totally debunk the possibility of such happenings. This shows just how much irrationality spans across human behavior.

Also, a school of thought is of the opinion that the reason for our continued irrationality stems from the nature of our will. This school, mainly characterized by philosophers, argues that the innate irrationality of our essence is responsible for the insoluble resistance stemming from cravings, actions, and thought patterns. Other opinions in support of this quote that regardless of the rationality expressed by people, the bane of existence arises from a will to do the irrational; totally defying any rational explanations.

Although this opinion seems rather oxymoronic,

what with the tendency of rationality amounting from irrationality, social scientists of human behavior have further proved true this claim. The perspective of social science considers human beings in their primary, natural states, as people of a vengeful, emotional, cognitive, narrow-minded, mistake-prone sort. This perspective somewhat rationalizes the state of the world with the natural state of its human populace. Social scientists opine that the world is as it is owing to the behavioral pattern of an irrational lot. This opinion drives home the point that, beneath the facade of rationality, irrationality prevails at the core of human existence and motivation.

Psychotherapists share an almost similar view on the concept of irrationality and human behavior. In psychotherapy, irrationality refers to the motive that influences the cognition, emotions, thoughts, and actions of a person towards a behavioral pattern, unreflective of the qualities of rationality. This behavioral pattern is characterized by a utopian, rigid, uncompromising, self-deprecating pattern of thoughts, which makes it most socially awkward and wreckful.

Factors That Influence Irrational Behavior

Regardless of the inherent nature of irrationality, it is capable of being triggered into expression by a host of factors, such as:

- **New Situations:**

People are more likely to act on impulse when faced with situations alien to them. And, since an impulsive act is never fully thought out, the subsequent response may likely be irrational. Learn as much as you can about that new job, new neighborhood or new team before diving into it. Also, take things slowly and allow your mind the chance to acclimatize to the new situations.

- **Stress:**

Be it physically, emotionally or mentally, people are inclined towards irrational behavior when they are worn out or exhausted. During these stressful moments, the mind's singular goal is to rest and regain lost energy. Whether you are aware of it or not, you simply want to breeze through discussions and all other situations which requires you to mindfully be present. Find some time in your schedule, however small, to rest and recoup your strength.

- **Peer Influence:**

As with the crowd mentality, peer influence is often the motivation behind irrational behaviors that an individual might not actually exhibit on their own. Take a societally established good kid, and place him or her with those considered to be bad. In little but a while, that kid would adopt the behaviors displayed by the group. You may think yourself too self-aware or intelligent to be swayed into anything against your will. Yet, even the smartest and those who are strong-willed still find themselves influenced by close friends, associates and people whose opinion they respect. Choose your friends like you do your dentist (if you are very picky about them, that is).

- **Intoxication:**

Under the influence of substances that 'mess up' mental and physical states, people tend to behave irrationally since they exercise no control over themselves. Little wonder law enforcers term it, 'acting under the influence.' Things take on a different texture and size for an intoxicated person. Words are spoken without any thought given to the consequences they would bring. When the chemicals in drugs and alcohol have waned from a person's bloodstream, they are likely to report feelings of shame and guilt for their earlier actions. This is even worse for those who are so given to abusing these substances, that they are now addicted. A simple solution to this would be that you do everything in moderate quantities and, when it has to do with drugs, under the advice and supervision of a licensed medical doctor.

- **Phobias:**

Phobias indicate an obsessive, irrational fear of certain things. People with a phobia for certain phenomena are likely to act in the most unthinkable, irrational way ever when introduced to their fears. Some reactions, in fact, of some people to their phobias bear curiously striking similarities to how one might behave upon seeing the devil himself. Even though the danger is mostly just imagined, the fear is very real. Their nervous systems kick into action, as it would in an actual life-threatening situation. Only those observing a person reacting to his or her phobias would know for sure the irrationality of their behavior. Limit your contact with things which spark up your phobias or visit a therapist for guidance on how to overcome these fears.

- **Anxiety:**

Anxiety denotes a distressing desire or uneasiness about something. When people become overly anxious, it results in anxiety disorders, which are influencers of irrational behavior. Unlike the other factors for irrational behavior which have been listed, people who suffer from anxiety disorders are usually aware that they are simply being irrational. Someone who has a problem making eye contact would imagine that they are causing others to be uncomfortable, despite knowing that this is far from true. People who are usually anxious in social gatherings might imagine themselves to be in the spotlight of everyone's glaring eyes. Try as they might to convince themselves otherwise, they would fail to shake off the crushing feeling. There are several tested drugs called Selective Serotonin Reuptake Inhibitors (SSRIs), which may be able to help people deal with their anxiety. Therapeutic methods include, psychotherapy and Cognitive Behavioral Therapy (CBT). If you suffer from anxiety of any kind, visit a psychotherapist to assist you in living your life to the fullest regardless of those irrational fears.

Chapter 6: Recognizing and Resisting Manipulation

Insomuch as you now have a working knowledge of how to play on the weakness of a person's psyche in order to manipulate it, it is also imperative you understand that you are not without your own weaknesses. Every human being grows to develop strengths in certain areas of their lives, but the sacrifice for this is the development of weaknesses in other areas. You may think that the better action would be to locate the places of weakness in our lives and deal with them, that we ought to spend the bulk of our lives making sure every part of our psychology, both mental and emotional, are strengthened against manipulation. But, this is a more stressful ordeal than to simply be able to recognize when someone is trying to manipulate you. Yes, the tables turn that quickly and there are those who would like to take advantage of the cracks in your psyche and get you to behave in their favor. As overly dramatic as this may seem, you would fall for them every time if you do not learn to recognize those situations.

You want to be the one playing on the emotions, fears, memories, and logicality of the next person, without having to fall prey yourself. There is no guarantee that the following tips will definitely protect against manipulative devices—you may not even want the ability to resist some people—but, what is certain is that you will be a step ahead of most people if you put them into practice.

Why We Are Easily Manipulated

Before getting into the ways of how to spot manipulation and how to resist being taken advantage of, it is useful to understand why it is that we can be manipulated. This goes beyond what our friends, families, bosses, businesses, and advertising agencies do. Do you know that many of the choices you make are not purely a product of your own will? Often, your conviction of a certain product comes from manipulation. Instead, your conviction stems from the banners, TV ads, and social media influencing. The question still remains, what in our psychology is so easily malleable that it can be bent by other people?

Our memories are one of the key areas that is played on, mainly by corporations with their advertisement campaigns. Over the years, we come to associate particular feelings of warmth, love, and nostalgia to certain items. The message of the adverts then promises satisfaction or relief if you purchase their products. They utilize songs, colors, drama, and other tools solely to this end. If properly done, we are less likely to fuss over the quality and price of that product and are more prone to buy it just for the sake of reliving a particular time when things were simpler and much brighter. We, in fact, go on to equate that brand to those feelings of nostalgia and deliberately seek them out from other, sometimes better, products.

Another reason we can be manipulated is that we worry about the consequences. We react to fear differently, with some of us having more control than others. To take advantage of this factor, people might drop hints as to the repercussions of refusing them. This is different from a threat or blackmail as the results of not giving in to their wants would be made to seem entirely of your own doing. Since we cannot determine the future, we try to stay on the safer side and choose what we perceive would have a lesser probability of blowing up in our faces. Sometimes, those who are trying to persuade or manipulate us into taking a particular action may not exactly suggest these consequences—if they do at all. Often, it is by our own thoughts that we push ourselves in the direction of their desires. We fear what could happen should we say no, and the fingers which would be pointed in our direction. We fear the shame of being wrong and choose instead to shift responsibility. In our minds, sometimes unconsciously, we decide that the fault would entirely be the other person's if we simply gave in and let them have their way. Unfortunately, it doesn't quite turn out as we imagined. We forget one important factor, our conscience; we would always be reminded that we could have chosen differently.

Yet another reason for this is our instinctive need be accepted by particular groups of people. You must have heard the saying that goes, 'no man is an island.' This is a very accurate description of human societal behavior. Even those with an introverted personality still would like to have a close friend they could discuss things with from time to time. We associate ourselves with cliques in school and join clubs later on in life for the same feeling of being a part of something. We fight against feelings of separation and long for connection. This is not necessarily a bad thing, but it very well could work against you, especially in situations where you have to negotiate with someone else. The sheer fear of being ostracized may well lead us into giving up whatever benefits could have been ours. You do not have to detach yourself from every human relationship in order to overcome this, but you must learn to feel complete on your own. We may want people to be in our corner, to get the inside joke, feel a part of something besides ourselves and have people root for us, but it is rarely ever the truth that we essentially need them. Learning to enjoy your own company, loving yourself, and being your own best friend are good steps to take in making sure relationships can never be used to manipulate you.

Being overly self-conscious and having little or no confidence in your abilities can open you up to manipulation. Such abilities could be anything from physical strength and talents to mental agility. If you do not believe in the things you can do, you will find yourself stuck in a continuous search for validation. It is often for this reason that otherwise intelligent individuals have been caught in very questioning situations. The problem with a reliance on other people to feel worthy is that no one really is perfect; perfection doesn't exist, since it is subjective to each individual. Most people are also in the quest to being the best version of themselves and, by so doing, may not be attentive to your need for validation. What is worse, is that those who notice this about you may recognize it as a weakness to be exploited; with them, there is always the promise (spoken or unspoken) of appreciation. They hold this kink in your armor as a kind of puppet string over you. While you continue in desperation to please these people, they enjoy manipulating you for as long as you can remain oblivious to it. It is not a fair thing on your mental and emotional health to be, or continue to be, in this position.

Now that we have some awareness regarding why our psychology can be taken advantage of by other people, let us get into the ways in which you can spot manipulation and how to resist them.

Spotting Manipulation

If you know someone who quickly falls into the habit of blowing an otherwise harmless statement completely out of proportion, then you just might have a manipulator on your hands. Their goal is to provide blanket explanations for a many-sided statement and paint you in an unflattering color. The more meticulous among them would do this to people who they perceive to be of the more soft-spoken kind. They know you would generally prefer to let things slide than spark up an actual confrontation and, in so doing, make you an accomplice in vilifying your personality.

People consider you in a different light from what you really are because you do not insist on your truth. The sad fact about this is we often have at least one such individual in our lives. They could be a family member or coworker, but you, unfortunately, have to live with them.

If you would like to share a space with them and

thrive regardless of these kinds of people, then you've got to learn the tricky art of reining your nerves and being vocal of your truth. In situations where all a third party has to go by is your word against the manipulator's, you cannot afford the expense of leaving your accusation and defense to one person. We are all of varied personalities and certain things come much easier to some than others, but you've got to learn to stand up for yourself. Keep explaining the nuances of your argument as many times as the manipulator tries to generalize them.

Have you ever been told that you have a terrible sense of humor? That you have just got to grow a thicker skin and learn how to take a joke? This might be true in some instances, but in many cases, this is just to further belittle you after making a callous joke at your expense. They often portray a cool and likable persona, which could make it hard to call them to order. Their charisma makes people support them with their cruel jokes while you have to maintain a facade.

You must keep a false appearance that says your feelings are not hurt or to avoid being labeled as temperamental.

To what end, you may ask? With you constantly being the butt of insensitive jokes, you find yourself trapped in a cycle of people pleasing. You make it a mission of sorts to be in their good books as a means of escaping the embarrassment. The only way to truly escape, though, is to call them out on it and separate yourself from their company. Seeing as they attract people to themselves, you may not want to feel like an outsider with no friends of your own, but the rewards are a reinforced confidence and peace of mind. You will, ultimately, find that it wasn't worth your energy to be associated with such people.

Another way in which a person might try to manipulate you is by attempting to distort your reality. No, not the conspiracy theories of mind control and other hypothesis of a matrix world; distortion of reality stated here refers to the ways in which a manipulator may try to shift blame, excuse their mistakes, and, generally, attempt to convince you that what you believe they have done and who you think they are is not the truth. Even when you become aware of their actions to coax you into giving in to them, they tell you that it is not what it seems. This is not even the usual defensive argument that is put up reflexively by people; they intentionally select words and use them persuasively to recreate your perception of them. You would often leave such conversations with a feeling of confusion. For example, if you hear these words spoken to you, 'come on, are you crazy? How could you think that? Grow up!' Then you must recognize them for what they are: Manipulation. Do not distrust yourself or doubt your mind. Often, things are exactly what they seem and you perceived them correctly. Be wary around people who would rarely, if ever, accept the blame for anything or try to make you the problem.

Resisting Manipulation

First, you need to be able to tell the difference between humility and being a sucker. Agreeing to every demand and falling prey to every attempt at manipulating is not a virtue worthy of being touted. Being sure about yourself and acting accordingly is anything but baseless pride. Sometimes, people only want you to walk with your head bowed so they can step all over you. Your reward for putting up with this kind of behavior would be their friendship, but, as has been mentioned earlier, it is not worth it. You truly are more valuable a human being than to be pushed about. Self-respect and dignity are the hallmarks of people who have found themselves and love what they see. This is not to encourage you into being full of it and behaving in exactly the same way as a manipulator; the point is that you place yourself in high regards and not let anyone make less of your skills and all-round personality.

Believe it or not, but pride is also one reason why a person would allow themselves be subjected to manipulation and ridicule. You want to be part of a clique and you don't want to be accused to be weak because you complain, so you take whatever harassment, insult, and deception is flung at you. Unfortunately, people are not blind to these things. You may assume they cannot see how you are pushed about and made the butt of the joke of every gathering, simply on the fact that they say nothing to you about it, but they do. Your weaknesses are made glaringly obvious, encouraging others to also take their chances at manipulating you. Keeping up a false appearance of strength is detrimental to your mental health and may prevent you from building honest relationships. Recognizes pride stems from shame and that the only way to stop it from ruining your life is to confront the manipulator and cut ties with them afterward.

It would be a disservice indeed to not mention that pretense is not the way to go. Having read that you should speak up for yourself and dissociate yourself from these toxic relationships, you may feel that you have to now pretend like your confidence is through the roof and you are totally impervious to any kind of hurt. Faking it is not effective for your mental or emotional health when you are still friends with the manipulator; it is also not helpful when you finally uncover the courage to break away from them. Truly work on yourself. Feed your mind with edifying content and meditate on all that is good about you and your life in general. There is no need to make believe you are something when that is not what you really are.

Finally, you must understand that you cannot be blamed for anybody's mistakes besides your own. We are, as they say, all creatures of free will. No one is without the ability to make choices and, as such, each person must take full responsibility for the rewards of their actions. Also, saying 'no' to anyone does not qualify you as a horrible person. If, after thinking about it, you do not believe that an action is the right one for that time, or you just have no faith in it, then feel free to politely decline. It is within your rights to choose these things for yourself and at no point should you be pressured into doing anything. Be self-aware and self-assured.

Chapter 7: Persuasion: Just How Wrong Is It?

We all know those people who can be very persistent about the things they want. When you find yourself in the uncomfortable position of arguing with them, it is often a wonder if at all they have ever heard the word 'no.' Their relentless persistence wears down your defense until you yield to their wants. Sometimes, this is done without any kind of malice attached, but there are those who still debate that being a persuasive individual is not a healthy characteristic. They see it as manipulation because anyone on the receiving end only gives in for the sake of relief. For others, it is an ability that everyone should possess in order to be successful because it aids in negotiation and marketing. Before we get to the end of this chapter, the hope is to provide a satisfactory answer as to how wrong it is to be persuasive. Also, as with manipulation, we will discuss the various ways to effectively persuade anyone.

Persuasion is often compared to manipulation because it involves influencing a person to take a decision that is different from what they had initially purposed to do. Differentiating these two concepts is somewhat tricky, even for psychologists. On the website, Psychology Today, Nathalie Nahai writes that 'the difference between persuasion and manipulation is intent.' She goes further to stress that, with manipulation, the person on the receiving end leaves with a feeling of remorse for having yielded to the manipulator's argument and that the case is not the same with persuasion. This sums it all up quite easily. People are often prone to making bad decisions, which can only be seen by the people around them. To convince them of this, one must apply persuasive skills.

The end goal of persuasion is often a win-win and, in many cases, only a win for the person who is being persuaded. This is what makes persuasion a more favored option to manipulation. It has no ulterior motives and does not use questionable methods to achieve its goal. Unlike the case of manipulation where you ought to create some distance between you and the manipulator, a person who goes through the trouble of persuading you to take a certain action most probably has the best intentions for you. This may not be your experience, but persuasion can be seen in the times when a friend would try to keep us awake to read for a test or to keep within the boundaries of a set diet. Or, in cases when they talk you into trying something new, simply for the fun of it. These, indeed, are honest cases of persuasion and the clear difference between it and manipulation becomes clearer with the examples.

We will now delve into different methods which can be utilized to persuade anybody.

The Methods of Persuasion

- One subtle way to persuade anyone is to

gently nudge them into reaching the same conclusion as you. This is considered the most effective of all the methods of persuasion. To do this, you should never suggest exactly what you would like to be done. You are to flirt about your main intent while dropping hints to guide them into, unknowingly, agreeing with you. This is most preferred in cases where the person you would like to convince would, otherwise, be adamant. If you can succeed at making them think they arrived at that decision on their own, there would be no need for further convincing and they would put in the needed effort to make it work since it is (from their perspective) their own idea.

- Give something to them in order to increase the chances that they would be persuaded in your favor. Like the point above this, do not be obvious about it. You may give it as a gift, which could serve as a preamble of sorts to introduce your point. At most, it would cause the other person to feel guilty and give in. This may be considered by some as bribing and, as such, a method of manipulation. But, it can only be a bribe depending on the nature of the situation. Also, as in the words of Nathalie Nahai, the difference is in the intention that propels it. If it is done as a kind of payment to facilitate an activity that would usually be considered criminal, then it is a bribe. What is implied with this tip is simply a way to hint at your point and help them to agree with you much faster.

- Incentives have always been a great way to get people on your side. Politicians use them during campaigns, and companies do not shy away from their effectiveness when they push a product. With an incentive, you are not merely bribing someone to do anything; the mode of operation is to make plain all that is in it for them. What are the rewards to be gained should they allow themselves to be swayed by your demands? This could be in terms of money or any other means they consider rewarding enough. For example, you could tell them how it would benefit someone they care for. In this way, you will succeed at getting them to feel as driven as you are concerning your proposal. Make sure that what you use as an incentive is something they care about enough for it to affect their decisions. You may think everyone is moved by money but, with respect to your demand, it just might not cut it. It is far better if there is some sentimental attachment towards your incentive.

- That wisdom is ancient does not have to make it outdated and useless for our time. Aristotle came with what he saw as the perfect formula to persuade anyone.

According to him, three factors must come into play for anyone to shift their stance on a matter. They were ethos, pathos, and logos. These Greek words refer to the credibility of an argument, how it appeals to emotions, and the logicality of it, respectively. Aristotle believed that if you could prove to a person that your argument is a genuine one, get them to see the benefits on an intellectual level, and tie them in emotionally, there is little chance that the person would not be persuaded.

- Get them on a 'yes' momentum before asking for what you want. What does this mean, you ask? The goal is to get them to agree with you on a number of topics before you bring in your main point. If you do this successfully, they would feel pushed to continue on the same pattern and say yes to you. You can do this by asking a question you know they would agree with and then saying, 'yes?' at the end. Do this repeatedly for a few minutes and then ask for what you really wanted. Human beings are creatures of pattern. Once it is established, we always feel prompted on a subliminal level to not break it.

- Urgency is another tool of persuasion that you could deploy. When you do not gift people the luxury of time to let your request be mulled over in their minds, they may feel pressured to respond immediately. Often, their decision would be in your favor. We see this every time with adverts and some of us have actually used it in the past, though without knowing it, to get things done. Have you ever been told that a discount would expire in less than a week, only to have it extended later on? During the 'final week,' you find yourself in a rush to get as much as you wanted while the discounts lasted. To make this work for you even better, use other methods of persuasion along with it. Tell whoever you are hoping to convince all they stand to gain, or lose, depending on their final decision. Then make them aware of the limited time involved and how important it is that they come to a decision quickly.

- How sure are you about your request? People, largely, can tell with what certainty you are speaking and will base their decision on this. It is especially true when they have little or no idea of what you are proposing. It is your resolve, then, by which they are convinced to agree with you. For instance, take a child who is yet to learn how dangerous something could be ... since they have never been hurt by playing with that object or engaging in that activity before, all they would have to go on would be the conviction with which their parents warn them of those things. This mentality does not change much as we grow older. During election campaigns, we are swayed more by the certainty in the voice of the politicians than anything else.

- Do not look down on the simplicity of having someone 'owe you one.' When you do someone a favor, they are likely to reciprocate this sometime in the future. Now, unless you want to lose a friend, do not demand, outrightly, that the favor is returned. Tact plays a major role in this method of persuasion. Simply asking should spark up the memory of when you came through for them.

- Pick your words with care, especially the first ones. Even though it is a popular saying that the best should be saved for last, what you say first is what will be placed at the fore of the memory of whoever you are speaking with. Objectivity is preferred by most people to judge the viability of any venture. As such, you are expected to talk not only about the advantages of whatever you are proposing but its drawbacks, too. This does not have to make your point any less solid or convincing. Persuasive people know to elaborate first on the pros and highlights of their proposals while carefully hinting at the cons. In so doing, the benefits of accepting your request will be too obvious to shake off.

- Do not fall into a long and boring speech, regaling people with the facts and figures of your requests. It is mostly unnecessary and should come when they ask questions about it or after they have accepted. You do not want people to zone you out in a conversation and leave you talking to yourself. Keep it brief, with carefully selected words to create the right images in their minds. Generally, shorter and more precise speeches are usually the most memorable ones. If done right, people may remember, verbatim, all you said and how you said it. Lengthy words, on the other hand, fall into the habit of being repetitive and, as a result, boring and of no effect.

- When the time comes for you to deploy those statistical facts and the overall technicality of your request, make sure you have them ready. This is to say, you should be well prepared before going to convince people about anything. Do your research to prevent the eventuality of appearing ignorant. It may sound corny to you, but rehearsing for meeting them would go a long way in not only bolstering your confidence but making sure you cover all your bases. Place yourself in the position of the person you are hoping to convince and imagine their possible responses. You will, in time, be able to correctly determine how they would receive you and your argument.

- It is never good behavior to speak above the heads of people; this is especially true when you need them to be on your side. It may be that you have been able to achieve, for yourself, more academic laurels than they have. Also, you may be older or, generally, just more informed than they are. This should not be the premise for your requests. It should, in fact, not be evident in the inflections of your voice or mannerisms. You may think to use those achievements as a means to persuade anyone, but as we have learned earlier in this book, the intent is what separates persuasion from manipulation. If it would leave your conversation partner feeling smaller or less sure about themselves, it cannot, honestly, be described as merely a persuasion technique. Talk with respect to them, regardless of their social status. After all, you would not be seeking their approval if they were not important to you.

- Have they done or agreed to similar things in the past for you or anyone else? If they have, then you may draw on this to strengthen your request. This also rests on the psychological fact that people are prone to repeat past behavior in order to continue that pattern. Remind them, at appropriate times in the conversation, of when they did a similar thing. This will be even more valuable to your case if those similar decisions did not hurt them and were full of benefits. Guide them on this train of thought with subtle prompts into arriving at the same decision, again.

- Sometimes timing is everything. The manner in which you will be received and how people will respond to your requests may very well depend on their mood in that period in time. There rarely is a perfect time to get anything done, but you study a person to determine their temperaments and take into cognizance the situation at that particular moment. It may not be sensible to broach a topic at a sensitive period, for example when a loss has occurred and the person you would like to request something of is grieving; in this instance, it would be more tactful to wait until the situation is less delicate. Also, you may observe that a particular person seems to be testier at certain times of the day; give your request the best chance possible of success by acting mindfully and choosing the right time to approach anyone.

- People in this day and age seem to enjoy the sound of their own voices, to the detriment of the formation of any meaningful and lasting relationship. Friendships and romantic relationships, today, seem to be superficial, at best. If you are going to persuade anyone, you have to listen; not an impatient silence that only waits for the other person to stop talking so they can begin their argument again. Listen to the objections of the other party carefully, as this would give you a better chance of persuading them. It would be impressed upon them that you truly care about their own thoughts and wellbeing and they are in turn likely to listen to you, raptly. People want to feel like they matter and you can achieve this by listening to them.

- What better way to get someone to agree with you than to hit them with your rich sense of humor. This should not be forced, though. If you aren't a naturally funny person or you find such things uncomfortable, then it may not be wise to apply this tip in persuading people. Whoever you are talking to will, very likely, notice your discomfort and the entire discussion may then seem too clinical to them. Go with who you truly are on the inside. This is to mean that your personality and abilities can be utilized to help you succeed at convincing people. Also, of importance is that you do not make jokes at the expense of the other person's happiness. Try not to go all out with trying to be so funny that you, unknowingly or not, insult them in the process. This is a kind of behavior that is expected of a manipulator and not a persuasive individual. The goal is simply to get the other person laughing so freely that they loosen up and allow themselves to be persuaded by you.

- And, when all else fails, we can certainly rely on the art of persistence. This is what a lot of people, generally, define persuasion as. If done right, without crossing the line into being full-on annoying, you will often get your wish by simply not backing down. The first decline does not, necessarily, have to send you away with your tail between your legs;

learn from each rejection and come back with a request that has been modified to cater for the nuances in the other person's behavior and the state of things at that moment. Be persistent without being incorrigibly annoying.

- You may have finally understood that persuasion is not, in itself, a bad thing and that there is an obvious distinction between persuasion and manipulation. The problem is that a lot of people find themselves leaping from one to the other. We all have those days in our lives when we want something rather desperately and for varying reasons, but at the time we suggest it to someone who is in a position to facilitate our request, they turn us down. This is no excuse to act with malice and take advantage of the weaknesses in those people. Do not blackmail or threaten them. Simply use any or all of the tips that are in this book. Proper research was conducted to verify the authenticity and efficacy of these tips and they are very likely to work for you. If, however, those people continue to turn you down and seem quite firm about it, then you should find another way to get what you want. Just do no resort to manipulative techniques or behave in such a way as to hurt anyone.

Chapter 8: Where Do our Opinions Come From?

Have you ever turned down a proposal simply on a hunch that it would fail? Have you met someone for the very first time and decided there and then that they weren't a good person? How about the conviction you have about certain values or the way you perceive yourself? It should nag your mind as to the actual origin of these opinions that have been so assimilated into our lives. In reality, none of the beliefs we have, regardless of how dear we hold them, are truly of our own creation. The external forces with which we must relate are what shape our opinions. Below are a few of these forces.

Society: This includes the family we are born into, the neighborhood in which we are raised, and our country at large. We, indeed, are but mere products of society's construct. As humans, the greater percentages of our personalities are formed while we are young (15-years-old and younger). At this time in our lives, we are usually very inquisitive, curious, and impressionable. We form close friendships, try out several things, whether they are forbidden or not, are challenged by popular opinions about life, the white, grey, and black sides to human psychology, and we seek for further answers on varying subjects when those provided by our parents do not suffice. It is from these raw materials that we form our own characteristic behavioral qualities and tendencies. This is not to mean that no one is unique; essentially, we are all different from each other. What this implies is that whatever our firm opinion on a matter is, it was and can be influenced by the society we live in.

Books: It is no secret that a nation is very likely to experience development that is proportionate to the state of their education system. Ponder on a country whose syllabus includes theories that have been proven wrong and are now considered outdated. Children who are under this kind of tutelage would mature into adults who are way behind on modern thoughts and opinions. Books, especially the hard copies, may be losing their popularity among modern people but they still wield such extraordinary influence over those who still have the patience and presence of mind to read one. Consider how romantic novels inspire imaginations and unrealistic expectations in the minds of their readers. Also, messages of hate and fear can be infused into a person from the pages of a book. These pages and pages of little more than words can grip the mind and create the believable illusion of being outside of this world and in another. With such power at their disposal, it is not a stretch to say that some degree of the opinions we claim to be ours stems from the books we have read.

Music: It is a common joke that people would be able to recall information they had read if it was made into a song. Scientifically, music has such an effect on the brain that both the right and left hemispheres can be seen to show heightened activity. The lyrics of our favorite songs may very well stay with us for the entirety of our lives and the messages in them play a vital role in shaping our opinions. It is little wonder then, that music is such an effective tool in influencing anyone to believe in a cause. Whatever myriad of emotions that man is bequeathed by, music has an answer for them. It can make us brave in times of fear, heals our hearts in times of grief, and also helps us deal with love. The more we search into the potential of music, we find the reasons why it is considered a weapon by some. It would be of immense help to us if we were more deliberate about our choice in music since we cannot bury our heads in the sand and pretend that music does not wield any control on our psychology.

Religion: The older we get, the more we wonder about the world around us. Questions arise that may seem baffling and overwhelming to even the brightest intellects among us. To quell the anxiety, which is born as a consequence of those, seemingly, unanswerable questions, we look to something higher and more powerful than ourselves. The various religions in existence are almost as numerous as the tribes and nations that practice them. These religions are often the foundation for the building of communities, laws, and societal norms. Wars have been waged, and are still being fought, simply because of disagreements on a one, true religion.

Since these religious beliefs are instilled in us from almost the second we are born, it is an almost impossible task to get anyone to change. Although religion often stops at the worship of a deity, it may go further to advise us on who to hate, be associated with, what is right and wrong, and the reasons for these rules. Even science and empirical thought are considered a religion by many people.

Chapter 9: Factors that Influence Human Behavior

Saying that sex sells, in this day and age, has become quite clichéd. Most people are aware that if any product–whether it's a toothpaste or hairbrush—is sexualized, it has a greater chance of reaching a wider audience and generating increased profits. The question, then, is why are we susceptible to be influenced by sexual content? What, in our psychology, makes us more willing to gravitate towards products containing implied erotic messages?

Loewenstein and Ariely conducted a social experiment in 2005, which revealed that men found it less difficult to show aggressive behavior when aroused. What can be taken from this study, is that poor decision making is more likely to happen as a consequence of being sexually aroused. This can be extended from the aggressive tendencies shown by the men in the above study to other kinds of decision making.

From favored products to our choice in life partners, sex is one factor that plays a more defining role than we know or would like to admit. Most of these sex-driven decisions happen on a subliminal level and this is why we are often oblivious to the fact that we can be swayed by even the most common innuendos.

Whether you agree with humanism or not, its view on the importance of sex for an individual seems to be reinforced every single time. It concludes that sex is the most basic desire in every human being and, by extension, implies that every other need revolves around this instinctive and fundamental drive for sex. If this is untrue, then why else has the pornographic industry experienced such a rise in popularity and in how much money they make? Even with the advent of free internet porn, this has not done much to put a dent in the financial prosperity of the industry. Other forms of entertainment are not left out of this; the music and movie industries are not known to shy from sexually explicit content to increase their viewership. Song lyrics, music videos, and even children's cartoons all incorporate some degree of sexual images for whatever purposes they deem fit.

It may seem like no big deal at all that sex has the potential to influence our purchasing decisions, but it gets much deeper and darker than that. While it cannot be said that the portrayals of sexual situations by pop culture celebrities in music and movies is entirely responsible for the increase in rape cases in many countries, it definitely does nothing to help the problem. In fact, it imprints unrealistic expectations, especially in the minds of young people. These forms of media cannot be said to be innocent from the increased proclivity of young adults to premarital and unprotected sex.

Advertisement agencies, being aware of this most basic desire in people, utilize sex to promote their products. We have seen models, sparingly clad, eating snacks with seductive and flirtatious body movements. There was also the video of a man ejaculating candies on his newly wedded wife. Though often not as glaring as the examples cited, they utilize the exact same power to influence our choices.

But, How Does Sex Influence Us?

The answer lies in three words: Attention, memorization, and repetition. Again, advertisement agencies know these things and have mastered the art of utilizing them. When you see an ad anywhere, the first that happens is that your attention is trapped for a duration of time. In order to not miss any of the provocative actions, you watch every frame raptly. During this time, the producers of this advert attempt to commit certain messages to your memory. For example, they might be trying to convince you about the superiority of a particular sportswear or energy drink compared to every other competition in the market, all the while promising certain rewards such as increased vibrancy or becoming the fancy of the opposite sex. Lastly, they use repetition to ensure that this message is duly ingrained into the cognitive processes of the viewers. When you turn on the television, use your phone or are driving to work in the morning, you will find yourself presented with this advertisement, which will further hammer down its message into your mind. When you next find yourself with a seemingly inexplicable preference for any particular product or brand, take a step back to think on the originality of that decision. You may find that you have no particular taste for such things and that your choice to purchase them has its basis in the sexual undertones of promotional videos.

Propaganda Influences Us

This is one word that is rarely spoken out loud. And when it is, people do so in hushed tones and at street corners or alleyways. You will find them constantly searching over their shoulders to make sure they are not discovered as their very lives could be at risk for saying 'propaganda.'

Propaganda is the repetition of any particular information that seeks to promote a cause or vilify another. It does not, necessarily, have to involve causes alone. Sometimes, the object of propaganda could be a person or an institution—again, to vilify them. Stories are readily available in the history books of how countries and civilizations of any structure used this tool in controlling the thoughts of their populace. It could even be used to convince people that laying down their lives for any particular cause will be more rewarding than anything they could have hoped for.

Whatever impression you have of propaganda, its power and reach have become even greater with the advent of technology. Being that leaders of nations can now get their messages to the citizens of their countries on social media, radio, and television, opinions of people can more easily be swayed without their knowing. More mastery has also been gained over propaganda and, as a result, these influencing messages are not as obvious as they once were. Subtle information can be slowly filtered to the general populace through controlled news outlets and other media sources.

The need for shortcuts in order to deal with the fast-paced world we live in is one factor that makes us susceptible to the influence of propaganda. We are often so focused on getting our own lives straight that we, unknowingly, acquire the need to have someone tell us who to love, hate, and how to behave in certain situations. Leaders who influence people by means of propaganda are not ignorant of the fact that poetry, music, and other art forms have the ability to shift a person's viewpoint and make them believe in an idea. Although it was a more common practice in times gone by for governments to utilize the power of art in order to manipulate the perspective of those in their charge, there is little reason to not believe that this has continued.

Propaganda-filled speeches are often delivered by

charismatic individuals who speak with quite a persuasive tone. Their messages are so meticulously prepared that it becomes too much of a chore for the Regular Joe to attempt to see past it. As much as you would like to think that your mind is more evolved as to be manipulated by lies, no matter how repetitive and sound, you must understand that sometimes these propagandas play into the latent emotions and beliefs inside of us.

Patriotism Influences Us

Love for, and loyalty to, your country play a determining role in how we relate to certain things and people; it is ingrained in us from a very young and impressionable age, and we carry this feeling for the rest of our lives. The hatred, love, fear or respect we feel for citizens of other countries may stem from the images that have been hammered into us, rather than from actual relations with these people.

As with the previous headers on influencing factors, patriotism may even affect things as basic as the products we purchase. If a particular good or service was created or offered from a country we are 'supposed' to feel some level of angst towards, we often do not bother to research the qualities they possess or how affordable they are. It may even register as insulting to us. Yet, patriotism may not always be in the usual sense of loyalty towards the country. Over time, we may feel this particular commitment towards certain institutions, brands or even cliques. From all that has been written to this point, it is obvious that people often make choices, not on the benefits involved but on the things we identify with and how they make us feel.

We are Influenced by Hate

How many times has a product harped on the popular dislike for their competitors in order to promote theirs as the better alternative? We are, sometimes, prone to make choices that are not based on merit but on our hateful feelings, instead. Also, someone else's hatred could very well become ours. This has been the reason for many wars and why some children grow up with a dislike for particular things, only to find, much later in life, an appreciation for those very same things. Although, some would argue that it is disinterest that stands as the opposite of love, and not actually hate; they say this to mean that hatred towards any one thing, or person, implies some affection for it, too. History, in any case, would beg to differ as the behavior of people towards those they claim hatred for, rarely, if ever, betrays affection of any kind. In fact, it cannot be said to be hate if it carries a soft spot for the object of this hate. The actions that arise from this feeling of hate are angry ones, which, in fact, border on being mindless.

It is not a common phenomenon that people would ask themselves why they hate what they proclaim to so hate. Should that happen, it just might be revealed that the reasons are not quite solid, however, that, most often, never happens. Instead, we exaggerate whatever injustice we may have suffered and allowed irrationality to take the driver's seat of our decision-making process. If it is a political party that has wronged us, we vilify the candidates from that party based on the actions, or inactions, of those before them and give room for the opposing parties to cash in on this feeling—even though they might not be as qualified.

And, it is only getting worse. Not only are there hate groups, but their numbers are ever increasing. In America alone, there are more than 900 of these specialized groups of people who bear similar hatred for particular things, institutions or people. And, as with almost every human vice, these hate groups have found their way into the internet and social media. There are Facebook groups created specially to allow people of the same hate, so to speak, vent their displeasure on the platform. Many of these groups contain as much as thousands of individuals, young and old, who regularly visit and participate.

This paints a picture of how much control we yield to hate. Our choices, decisions, actions, and even health can all be influenced by this much hate that we feel. We must learn to separate what we feel from what we stand to gain and choose logically.

How to Conquer the Influence of Hate

Hate refers to a strong feeling of repugnance or dislike. Hate, like its alternative other, love, is one of the strongest emotions there is. It is a feeling that human beings deal with regularly, one that's capable of influencing behavior. Hate is able to influence behavior owing to its complex structure, which combines anger with judgment. This breakdown makes its influential nature quite understandable because anger is an emotion directed at a person or thing and judgments arise subsequently from thinking about the object of anger. Ironically, judgment fosters anger, which accounts for why hate isn't an easily eradicated emotion.

Hate is, doubtlessly, one of the greatest motives that have ever propelled people into a line of action, either as a response or a cause. History itself carries many different stories of hate and its subsequent results that aren't uncommon even in contemporary times. For example, during the peak of racism and white superiority, black people suffered at the hands of white people for no other crime than the color of their skin. Other than this, there existed no other rational reasons as to why black people were victimized, other than sheer hatred. As an emotion of response, history also has stories of victorious rebellions all birthed from hatred.

This shows just how much hate can stem from a variety of reasons that may not necessarily be rational, but thrive nevertheless. Hatred has been known to emanate from the littlest incidences such as frictions in interaction, to more neutral scenarios such as differences in religion, and finally to complex situations such as heartbreaks or wickedness.

Regardless of the reason, hate is an emotion dangerous to both the physiology of the hater and to society at large. Research has shown that hate is toxic to the physical and cognitive states of an individual. Experts are of the opinion that hate could sometimes be responsible for reduced levels of immunity and higher susceptibilities to diseases. In this regard, it is thus important that one conquers the influence of hate on them as an individual.

In itself, the influence of hate cannot be put away outrightly, because it exists in different measures across people and has a somewhat higher tendency to be triggered by certain factors. However, its influence on behavior can be stemmed down considerably through the following means:

1. Understanding the Complex Nature of Hate

As earlier mentioned, hate comprises of anger and judgment. To successfully reduce the influence of hate on an individual, the very buildup of hatred must be considered distinctly. This is because its primary components offer an insight into the cause of the hate and to whom or what it is directed at. This, in turn, helps demystify the hatred, making it capable of being understood and possibly resolved.

The first step here is to identify the cause of the hate, which denotes the person or thing it is being directed at. This step forms the basis by which hate can be interpreted and critiqued, based on the judgments expressed. Here, studies suggest that emotion can be conquered by inquiring into the reason and nature of the hate. That is, the authenticity and rationality of the hate should be considered. While this may seem rather strange, studies opine that hate can, in fact, be conjured up by imagination, or triggered by irrational feelings. This would account for why people can hate others for absolutely no reason.

For example, it is not uncommon phenomenon to see people hate others on account of their wealth, affluence or position of power.

2. Letting Go

Hate wouldn't always be the lightest, easiest thing to let go of or forget, but understanding the negative impact of hate on the lives of people and society can help this course. Religion and other sects even propagate the notion that forgiveness is essential in overcoming hate because holding on to is as good as 'eating poison and expecting another person to die,' as a maxim rightly puts it.

Forgiving and forgetting the source of hate is key in letting go of hatred in order to escape the physical and emotional damage that might be incurred from the negative emotion. You might argue that letting go is one of those many suggestions which fall into the category of, 'easier said than done.' When someone has broken the trust we had in them or failed us in any way, it truly is an ordeal to patch things up with them and put the hurt from your mind. Think of it instead as doing yourself a favor. Life has a way of putting us in positions where we need, not only who we least expected, but who we would rather not be associated with ever again. Social situations like this can be quite the discomfort unless you make peace with those who have hurt you. It's a freeing way to go about life.

3. Empathy

Some like to claim that it just isn't in them to be empathetic, but, in truth, everyone has this potential. If you only tried, you will find that you have the ability to see things from the other person's perspective. It becomes much harder to hate anyone when you understand why they behave the way they do. But, empathy is more than simply understanding the other person's viewpoint. In its broadest sense, it refers to being able to feel what the next person is feeling. This is an upgrade on sympathy, which only feels sad for the person. With empathy, if someone feels sad, then you also feel sad with them. Only feelings of love and respect can be born from cultivating empathetic habits. Regardless of how vile the person you hate is, or what level of hurt they have caused you, you realize that they are as human as you are. It is much easier to forgive a person when you can relate to them on a more humane level. This is because we objectify and vilify people when we hate them. If you can feel empathy for them, continuing to hate them would feel quite the same as hating your very own self. It may be hard to practice this, but it is humane and worth a try.

4. Talk to Them

When you hate someone, it is expected that the last thing you want to do is to talk to them. You would much prefer to put as much distance between you and that person as you can possibly manage. But, if it is your goal to kill the hatred and instead make friends, then you should create the opportunity for a sit down with that person and really talk to them. Usually, when tempers are not flaring and insensitive words are not being thrown about, you will find that anyone can be likable. True, there are some who work very hard at being exceptions to this rule, but it is up to you to give people the benefit of the doubt before judging them. When you decide to talk to them, make sure you do not go into the meeting with a hateful attitude. Your initial opinions on the person were formed out of distaste for what they had done, what they represent, the things you had heard about them, and so on. When you meet with them, make it feel like it is the very first time and you also want to create a good impression. Treat them with respect and give a listening ear to their side of the story. Friendships born from these kinds of situations are usually the best kind.

5. Change Your Focus

Mostly, the opinions we about people in our minds depend on the angle from which we view them. The people you consider friends and that you love without bounds are who others see as enemies. People who see you walking and laughing with your friend(s) may wonder why you would associate yourself with that caliber of person. Yet, these friends can do no wrong in your eye. It all depends on where your focus is. It really has little to do with the people themselves. If you would practice this consciously with everyone you meet, you may find that no one is truly worth hating. Human beings are very complex animals and there is never one side to our personalities. The same person you hate may very well possess the same qualities you admire. The question is, are you willing to make the effort to see beyond your hatred? It often turns out that those you hate, in fact, like you. Yet, even if that is not the case, having a good feeling towards everyone you meet does more for you than it does anyone else. You will feel more at peace with yourself and it helps your health in ways medicine can only dream of.

6. Allow Time

Time, sometimes, is really all that is needed to make things clearer. If someone has made you angry or has hurt your feelings in any way, it is not the best thing to act on it immediately. If you vent your anger or behave in a vengeful manner, you may feel the compulsion to continue acting in the same manner towards that person. Assuming there is no immediate and pressing need for the matter to be resolved, you would continue in this pattern until you just hate that person simply from habit. When you start feeling those symptoms of anger—your heart rate increases, your palms get sweaty, your tongue feels salty, your vision takes on a different quality—sit down and breathe in, deeply. Think of totally unrelated things and allow the moment to pass before getting up and talking to that person. During that waiting time, you may also think of the good aspects of that person. If they have ever come through for you in any way, let your mind munch on those. When you decide it is time to talk to them again, make sure it is not from a place of judgment or anger. When people feel confronted, the instinctive behavior is to act defensively. If you challenge them with hateful words, they are very likely to respond in the same way. This is not helpful for anyone. Allow time to do its job.

7. Set Boundaries

This is more of a preventive action than anything. If you do not set the limits of interactions between you and anyone else, lines would be crossed unknowingly. Let people know, in clear terms, the things that irk you. If you do not appreciate a certain pattern of behavior around you, don't behave contrarily just because you want people to like you. When they hurt you without meaning to, your reaction may then be to hate them. This really is not fair to anyone involved. The question then is usually, how to ask people to stop acting a certain towards or around us without hurting their feelings. First, your emotions are just as important as theirs. You may have heard the saying that, the freedom of any individual stops right where someone else's begins. It is only with such a mindset that healthy relationships, devoid of hate, can be fostered and maintained. Secondly, those who care about you, without ulterior motives, will actually appreciate it when you speak out and inform them about the things which do not sit well with you. No one wants a friend they care for to simply put up a façade of happiness, while they boil inside. A person's joy should not come at the expense of those around them. Speak up and set boundaries. If you lose a friend in the process, then they likely were not really your friends to begin with. Otherwise, you will earn the respect of your friends and family.

Chapter 10: Fear and How to Overcome Its Influence

Fear is a common motivator for the choices we make in life. We are prone to worrying about the variables in life which are outside our control and as a result, we act out. The more commonly discussed flight or fight responses in human beings, to situations of danger, are an example of the influences of fear. From the individuals we choose to vote for during elections to what kind of activities we engage in, we are driven by this reflex action to make decisions. Having explained all that, living in this way poses a problem: One is more likely to make a poor and detrimental decision if it rests on fear alone

Fear makes no provisions for the application of common sense, which, in turn, leads to irrational behavior and bad consequences. Guess who understands and applies this to their marketing campaigns? That's right, advertisement agencies. Ever heard of flash sales? How about discounts that only last for a short while? The 'get it now or never' syndrome pushes the buyer to quickly purchase the goods or services without much of a consideration. After buying the product, though, the buyer may then begin to have regrets about the purchase as the adrenaline slowly leaves their bloodstream. For some reason, things appear to be of more quality if they are almost sold out or are in limited edition.

You must learn to master self-control if you would have any chance of not being moved by fear. Have you ever been in situations where a group of people is running from a perceived danger and you join them in running towards the same direction even though you have little idea of what the threat is? It may be that you have never found yourself in this scenario, but you must have heard of something similar happening. This is probably left-over behavioral traits from our prehistoric ancestors, but it's one that is hard to shake off. It is this same characteristic that is banked on individuals and establishments to get us to behave in a certain way. We feel unsafe with the minority and believe that if a lot of people are doing any particular thing, then something must be right about it.

Our individuality makes this a shaky foundation on which to base our choices. Since no two people are exactly alike, it goes without saying that no two people will agree on everything or prefer the same things. And, the riding on the fact that the majority of people opt for a certain product does not ensure that it would also be a good fit for you. Take the differences in introverts and extroverts in the world, for example. According to statistical evidence, there are more extroverts than there are introverts. These terms, extrovert and introvert, need little explanation as they are commonly thrown around. In simple terms, extroverts are the more outspoken and outgoing individuals who generally prefer to be at the center of any gathering. The introverts, by definition, are the polar opposites. They much prefer their own company, would rather be indoors and, generally, keep to small circles of friends. Going by this example, to say that a decision is the correct one because the majority opts for it would mean the same as introverts making the same choices as extroverts. Yet, it is a message promoted in many adverts to cash in on this fear of being with the lesser of the population. They will tell you how most people have chosen their product and may even show proof of how their popularity has grown. This does not make it a good premise for decision making.

Overcoming the Influence of Fear

Since it is not constructive to point out a problem without posing solutions to it, here are some ways in which you can deal with fear and stop it from controlling your choices and, by extension, your life. Some of them might appear too easy to actually be effective, but you ought to learn to give things a shot before concluding on them.

1. Distraction:

We, unconsciously and reflexively, practice this when we are confronted with a crisis. You may have been in a dangerous situation where it seemed imminent that something bad would happen. Maybe you screamed at that point or shut your eyes tightly; those were distraction techniques. Yet, to gain control over your fears and conquer them, you would have to learn to distract yourself with intent. Look away from the object or situation that inspires fear in you and critically assess the problem. You may find that things are not as dire as you have imagined them. Distraction affords you the opportunity to stop yourself before you act irrationally. Continuing to look at or think on the object of your fear only serves to trigger the flight or fight response that is still very present in the psychology of every human being.

2. Do Something:

If you continue to back away from your fears, their hold over your life becomes increasingly stronger and may haunt you for as long as you are alive. On the other hand, when you brave your fears, you would often find that they are not as menacing as you have constructed them in your head. How much progress in modernity do you reckon man would have been able to achieve, had they given up because of fear? There is no promise that you will have a life devoid of times when fear would wrap itself around you and make you just want to curl up somewhere and stop everything. But, you must exercise your free will and keep going despite fear standing before you. Take action by learning and practicing. Imagine that, for whatever reason, your kitchen is on fire. Freaking out at this point may not do you much good. Instead, you should reel your fears in and deliberately start applying all you have learnt on how to stop fires. Determine the level of the fire to know if your fire extinguisher will be able to handle it or call the fire brigade. This is an apt example on how you should do something regardless of your fears.

3. Eat the Right Things:

There are a few points wrapped up in this single tip, and we will take them one after the other. First, your diet has more impact on your reaction to life's challenges. You may have heard that the consumption of sugar can be addictive and, in turn, can produce feelings of depression in those who abuse them. Some might even consider this to be far worse than being addicted to hard drugs because very few people are aware of its addictive capabilities and consider it mere food. Besides depression potentially being caused by sugar consumption, a careless diet can also decrease our self-control in times of stressful situations. When you are ashamed of how much weight you have gained and are not comfortable in your own skin, this could eat away at your self-confidence. You may then feel forced to always back down at the slightest hint of risk. Lastly, the information you feed into your mind goes a long way in determining how you stand against your fears. If you are constantly around people who only talk about their incapability and how tough life is, you will react with cowardice every time. Remember, society is an influencing factor whether we choose to accept it or not. Watch videos, listen to songs and have mentors who advise on standing your ground regardless of the problem. Even though fear does have its place in warning us about danger and protecting us from harm, if you yield your life over to its control, you will never be able to achieve real success.

4. How Do You View Things?

In short, this refers to your perspective. Anything can look big or small, depending on the angle you are looking from. If you view a problem with pessimistic glasses on, it would be nearly impossible for anyone to convince you of the positive possibilities. Thankfully, humans can learn new things just as they can unlearn unproductive and outdated ones. Teach yourself to always don a positive mindset. Most times, how things turn out in the end relies mostly on how we behave, rather than on the actual gravity of the problem. If you allow things to overwhelm you with ease, do not be surprised or blame life when you find yourself at the bottom. Always remember that, as a human being, you have the tools needed to rise above any problem: Free will and a mind. Use them to flip the odds, however daunting, in your favor. It is possible.

5. Learn to Take a Step Back:

This doesn't mean that you should back down and allow yourself to be swayed by fearful emotions but that you should separate yourself from your fears. Fears have a way of wrapping themselves about us and we, in turn, may assimilate them. It then becomes an ordeal of sorts to be aware outside of these fears. Our fears have the ability to convince us, on a subliminal level, that we are nothing outside them. If you would take a step back and meditate on all the nuances of your personality, you may find that you are more courageous than you knew. Think of the people who are rooting for you to succeed and, if there aren't any, then encourage yourself with the fact that some of the greatest people to have lived had no one but themselves. This means that you can be enough for and be complete in yourself if you would take out the time and put in the effort to reorient yourself with this belief.

6. Ask Questions:

Luckily for us, we are living in an era where the right to speak is mostly respected and, depending on what country you are living in, you will not be killed for asking questions. What then could be your excuse for allowing yourself to be shrouded in the cold darkness of ignorance? This is often the seed for a life of fear. Human beings still carry the genes that advise us to be wary about the things we have no knowledge of (have you seen depictions of cavemen discovering fire?). The moment we have gained enlightenment on the subject, we automatically become powerful over it. We find that if we know about something, then we can control it. And, if we can control it, there is little need to live in fear about that thing anymore. Do not continue with the school of thought that preaches ignorance to be bliss. In truth, ignorance creates the illusion of bliss by making us afraid to try new things.

7. Failure is Not Who You Are:

Your failures in life do not happen as a result of who you are but because of the things you did, did not do at all or didn't do enough of. This is why it is dangerously erroneous to term anyone a failure. That you have failed at anything is not a testament to who you really are but a prompting for you to put more effort into doing the needful. Instead of putting yourself down and hammering down a belief of inadequacy in your subconscious, work harder at gaining the useful skills that are a prerequisite to success in whichever area you need it. If you would make sacrifices of your time, energy, and abilities, you will be sharing the same testimonies as those you have grown to look up to.

8. Failure Is Not an Anomaly:

As ironic as it may seem, running from failure could very well mean the same as running from success. If you are too afraid to fail that you never try anything besides the usual, you will often find yourself at the same spot every year. Go out of your comfort zone and try the seemingly impossible. So what if you fail? The best recipe for a successful life, very often, includes ingredients of failure. It is from those failed tries, the ones you call mistakes that you could learn the best and most effective way to go about it, should you decide to try again. Famous success stories do not come without a few failed attempts, but we only learn of those who keep trying and never give up or stop believing. The names of those who give in to fear and quit are lost in the sands of time.

9. The Power of Helping Others:

Have you ever tried to teach someone a subject you are not so strong at, only to have it further etched into your memory? It is the simple way in which our minds are designed to assimilate things. This can be applied to assist you in getting over your fears. How? Help someone get over their own fear, which may or may not be similar to the one which confronts you. It really is that simple. By encouraging people and offering advice on how they could conquer their fears, the same is instilled in you and you may find yourself applying them before you become aware that you are. Before you start to worry that this would simply be a case of hypocrisy, the main idea here is not for you to lie about having things that scare you. Simply be a listening ear and teach them what you have learned from reading this book. In the end, you will find that it is not a mere saying that we rise by lifting others.

10. **Just Relax:**

It works as powerfully as it sounds basic. Sometimes, the challenges we face are not nearly as grave as we escalate them to seem. One of the best ways to deal with them is simply to chill and let your heart rate return to normal. Fear has the potential to adversely affect our health and as such, we ought to learn to breathe easy. Calming yourself down in the heat of the moment allows your brain to think up solutions with ease. Anxiety and constantly fidgeting about the future, which is beyond our comprehension or control, leads to poor decision making. It is a feat indeed to apply our minds to the best of its potential when it is clouded by fear. It was mentioned earlier that fear keeps us safe by making us aware of the danger and helping us make quick and on the spot decisions, but the things we decide in those moments are impulsive at best and may lead to regrets when we are relaxed enough to analyze them. Take charge of your mind, body, and soul. Choose how you will react to whatever is thrown at you and keep a calm and rational head, regardless of the situation.

11. Count Your Blessings:

These three words do more than simply make up the lyrics of an old church hymn. The simple application of the principles hidden in them can go a long way in enriching our lives. This is because a great number of the things which make us afraid are not the usual life or death situations. Often, it is our worry about the unknown which gives rise to fear. We worry about the things we don't have, the people who just seem to have it in for us, the influential personalities we are not connected with, the many information we do not have, and how all of these might derail or prevent our success and happiness. You must remind yourself, as often as possible, that worry is not a factor which makes good things happen faster. In fact, it compounds the problem by taking from the quality of your health and stops your mind from functioning optimally. A good way, in times like these, to gain a firm handle on your wandering mind is to think instead on the good in your life. What blessings are you thankful for? What learned skills or natural abilities do you possess? Do you have love in your life? Do you have a job? Are you enjoying good health? We all have, at least, one of these to be grateful for. Let your mind settle on them. Let them be the fuel you need to keep on moving despite the daunting nature of the challenges you face. Count your blessings, name each one and ruminate on them.

Conclusion

This book was written with the singular goal of helping people gain more control over their lives and equip them with the knowledge of how to persuade anyone. You should now be aware of the several ways you can analyze an individual to know how they are feeling, that you can tell the differences between manipulation and persuasion, the several factors that influence our choices and how to overcome fear and. Utilize the knowledge shared in this book to ensure your immunity against manipulation. Make your choices your own and not the result of people influencing you against your will. The several ways in which they can accomplish this have been revealed in this book and very little has been kept from you. This should not deter you from reading other material on the subject, but the research that was carried out and meticulousness put into writing this book ensures that it is balanced and touches all the salient points. Also, make new friends and try new things as you live above hate and fear. Opportunities await you at almost every corner, but fear and hate may blind you to them. Hate prevents you from having a healthy relationship with people who may be of help to you. It also causes you to judge with harshness and irrationality individuals who, otherwise, could have been close friends with you. Fear, on the other hand, holds you back from going after your dreams and making progress in any field. Fear would whisper in your ears that if it is uncharted territory, then you must stay away from it. Yet, these two emotions need to be placed under control for you to live a productive life. If you have found the contents of this book to be of help to you, then do not hesitate to share it with your friends and whoever you believe would benefit from reading it. Congratulations on the time you have sacrificed to read this book. The information herein will come in handy as you navigate the rough waters of life. Now, go out there and conquer.

www.ingramcontent.com/pod-product-compliance
Lightning Source LLC
Chambersburg PA
CBHW030111100526
44591CB00009B/369